Praise for
*Raising Successful Teens*

"Raising teenagers has never been easy—but these days it's more challenging than ever! With the prominence of social media, self-harming, substance abuse, sexting, and an alarming array of other trends placing today's youth at risk, parents are desperate to help their children navigate our post-Christian culture. In his new book Jeffrey Dean not only assures moms and dads that it's possible but also provides a wealth of practical suggestions for raising teens who embrace biblical truth."

—JIM DALY, president of Focus on the Family

"*Raising Successful Teens* is a must-read for today's Christian parents. Jeffrey Dean's message is encouraging and empowering, but more importantly, it is practical. He provides proven advice for how parents can raise teens who love God and live wisely in an ever-changing world."

—JOSH D. MCDOWELL, author

# RAISING SUCCESSFUL TEENS

### How to Help Your Child
### Honor God and Live Wisely

# JEFFREY DEAN

**REVISED AND UPDATED EDITION**
Previously published as *The Fight of Your Life*

MULTNOMAH

*For my wife, Amy.*

RAISING SUCCESSFUL TEENS

Details in some anecdotes and stories have been changed to protect the identities of the persons involved.

Trade Paperback ISBN 978-0-525-65324-0
eBook ISBN 978-0-593-19274-0

Copyright © 2019 by The Jeffrey Dean Company, LLC

Cover design by Mark D. Ford

Published in the United States by Multnomah, an imprint of Random House, a division of Penguin Random House LLC.

MULTNOMAH® and its mountain colophon are registered trademarks of Penguin Random House LLC.

Library of Congress Cataloging-in-Publication Data
Names: Dean, Jeffrey, author.
Title: Raising successful teens : how to help your child honor God and live wisely / Jeffrey Dean.
Other titles: Fight of your life
Description: Second Edition. | Colorado Springs : Multnomah, 2019. | Rev. ed. of: The fight of your life : why your teen is at risk and what only you can do about it. 1st ed. 2009. | Includes bibliographical references.
Identifiers: LCCN 2018059363 | ISBN 9780525653240 (pbk.) | ISBN 9780593192740 (electronic)
Subjects: LCSH: Parenting—Religious aspects—Christianity. | Parent and teenager—Religious aspects—Christianity. | Christian teenagers—Religious life. | Christianity and culture.
Classification: LCC BV4529 .D425 2019 | DDC 248.8/45—dc23
LC record available at https://lccn.loc.gov/2018059363

Printed in the United States of America
2019—First Edition
Previously published as *The Fight of Your Life*

10 9 8 7 6 5 4 3 2 1

SPECIAL SALES
Most Multnomah books are available at special quantity discounts when purchased in bulk by corporations, organizations, and special-interest groups. Custom imprinting or excerpting can also be done to fit special needs. For information, please email specialmarketscms@penguinrandomhouse.com.

# Contents

# Introduction

I met fifteen-year-old Kallie several years ago. I know she loves Jesus and really wants to honor Him with her life. She is popular at her high school and with students in her church youth group. However, she found that the line between right and wrong began to blur in a new dating relationship. I heard her story from a friend who had borrowed Kallie's phone to make a call. While using Kallie's phone, the friend noticed nude pictures of Kallie. The friend also noticed that Kallie had sent some of the photos to her boyfriend.

When the friend asked Kallie about it, Kallie confessed that she sent the pictures after several requests from her boyfriend. (By the way, this is the new cool in our culture: taking off your clothes, snapping a picture, and hitting Send. If you believe your teen is immune to such choices, you are wrong.) In this instance, a Christian teenager who knows better chose to cater to her boyfriend's wishes rather than honor God. Now the images are on her boyfriend's phone and potentially could be shared with his friends or posted online. Kallie's boyfriend made a wrong choice when he encouraged her to compromise her character. Their mistakes could be costly to them in a number of ways.

Kallie is one of many young people who believe that sharing nude selfies is the equivalent of sending an innocent love letter. Her boyfriend is one of a multitude of teenagers who believe that requesting and receiving nude pictures from a girl is just a normal part of life for Generation Z. Kallie and her boyfriend are part of a generation that has been bombarded with lies, and they are desperate for truth.

Like many teen girls I meet, Kallie longs for acceptance. Meanwhile, her boyfriend is willing to give up his integrity (and Kallie's) to satisfy his lustful desires. Many teens won't encounter this exact situation, but they *will* encounter equally consequential choices. Dealing with Satan's lies is every teenager's daily reality.

As I speak to students around the country, I hear stories you wouldn't believe. Satan is determined to destroy every teen, without exception (see John 10:10). You likely remember the challenges you faced in your teen years. Temptation has always been there, and the Enemy has always been the same destroyer he is today. It is important to note, however, that the internet and the proliferation of mobile devices intensify the battle our kids are in. Teens are overwhelmed by information, anything-goes (or lack of) ethics, and the inevitable experimentation that results. For Generation Z teens, the world moves at a pace you and I never would have dreamed was possible.

Every week teens write to me about addictions to social media, video games, and pornography. I talk to many teens and parents who tell me they have a friend, family member, or classmate who is addicted to prescription drugs. By the time students are graduating from high school, most tell me they have consumed alcohol and been offered drugs. Some states have legalized the use of recreational marijuana, and more appear to be following that lead. Most teens say marijuana is easily accessible, legal or not.

In addition, several states now offer a third legal gender option on birth certificates and other state documents. More states will follow, allowing anyone eighteen or older to change their current "male" or "female" designation to "X"—meaning they choose not to be on record as male or female.

Just this week I talked with people about issues related to sexual identity, pornography, failed relationships, suicide, divorce, self-harm, depression, and sexting. Even more than with past generations, it seems there is no end to how far this generation of teens will go to address their needs, curiosity, and desires.

A parent told me, "My husband and I learned that our tenth-grade son is questioning his sexuality. He revealed his desire to dress like girls, and he thinks he is attracted to boys. Our son is a Christian, is heavily involved at church with the youth praise band, and has said for years that he wants to work in missions after college. We are questioning everything we did as parents and are wondering where to go from here." I receive email and Facebook messages every week from parents who are overwhelmed by the reality that a son or daughter is struggling with gender-identity issues.

"These are the ways of the world: wanting to please our sinful selves, wanting the sinful things we see, and being too proud of what we have. None of these come from the Father, but all of them come from the world" (1 John 2:16, NCV). Our number one enemy works overtime to convince our kids that pleasing their sinful natures isn't sinful. As this verse reminds us, Satan deceives them into believing that sinful things they become aware of are things they need. As a parent, you are positioned to help your teen sift through the deceptions so he can embrace truth.

Countless students have been lost in the madness. However, I know many who have risen above life's struggles and temptations and chosen the way that is right and good and God honoring. Read what Claire, the mom of a high school junior, told me:

My son Kendell has been through it and back again! If it's out there, he has probably tried it a time or two, or two hundred. He's been in jail, been kicked out of two schools, already has a daughter, and is only a junior in high school. Through it all, my husband, Craig, and I have never given up on him. A year ago, we specifically began to pray Proverbs 16:3: "Commit to the LORD whatever you do, and he will establish your plans." We prayed this prayer all the time. And God did a miracle in Kendell's life. Kendell began to change. I can't explain it, but he did.

We are now on the other side of his former lifestyle, and he is a new young man! He's had to face some pretty steep consequences, some of which will remain for a lifetime. But a new set of friends, a new school, and Kendell's new commitment to give God (and his family) another try has made all the difference. We are living proof that you can never give up on your kids!

The psalmist wrote, "Guide me in your truth, and teach me" (Psalm 25:5, NCV). This is the rally cry of your teen's heart. What a privilege you have as a parent to guide your child to truth.

## The Privilege of Parenting

My wife, Amy, and I received a phone call from a neighbor who told us his baby son had died at delivery. Our neighbors finally had conceived a child after trying for several years, but during the baby's delivery, something went horribly wrong. A year has passed since this tragedy. The parents are still devastated.

Many people such as my neighbors would give almost anything to be a parent. I can't explain why God chooses to give children to some and not to others. But knowing that He has chosen me, I do not take the call to parenting lightly. You shouldn't either.

God never would have given you the privilege of being a parent if He didn't have an awesome plan for you. He has given you everything you need to be the exact parent your teen needs. This book will help you become the parent you were made to be.

I will first discuss what it means to study the culture in which your teen lives. That will prepare you to keep your eyes open so you can be armed and alert. I will talk about your greatest strategy, which is to use God's Word. And I will call you to pray. James 5:16 reminds parents that "the prayer of a righteous person is powerful and effective."

I will also talk about what your role does not include. It's not your responsibility to prop up your teen or to save your son or daughter. Rather, you are to teach discernment and provide a solid foundation from which your teen will learn to live from a biblical perspective.

Last, I will discuss the incredible privilege you have been given to encourage your teen to live wholeheartedly for our lord and savior, Jesus Christ, the one who is greater than anything this world can throw her way.

Here are five critical foundational truths:

1. You are the most influential person in your teen's life—more so than any friend, coach, teacher, pastor, boyfriend, girlfriend, or celebrity. I hear this regularly from teenagers. So consider this: How are you influencing your child?

2. Your teen wants you to be involved in his life. Contrary to the lie of Satan and regardless of the many times your teen rolls his eyes before storming out of the room, he wants you to be an involved parent.

3. No matter what is culturally accepted, nothing is more authoritative than the truth of God's Word. It is up to you to communicate His truths to your family. Don't allow yourself to be swayed by rules, values, and assumptions that come from any source other than the Bible.

4. You are a parent, not a pal. Teenagers don't need their parents to be their friends; they need them to be parents.

5. You have to be willing to enter into discussions that make you uncomfortable. No matter the fallout, you have to go there when it comes to difficult, risky, or potentially awkward topics. You need to be the constant voice of reason and truth, the adult who is willing to talk about anything and will compromise nothing.

Parenting is likely the toughest job you will ever have. On some level, all teens will encounter every issue we'll discuss in the chapters that follow. You need to be equipped. I want to help you become the parent God has called you to be.

Over the past twenty-six years, I have counseled many parents, including expecting parents, single parents, parents of one teen, parents of multiple teens, parents of girls, parents of boys, and parents of both girls and boys. Though each story differs, I have had the privilege of meeting so many parents who desperately want the best for their children. I have included many of their stories in this book, and I know you will be encouraged and challenged as you read.

For the purposes of clarity, consistency, and simplicity, I have chosen to write this book in terms of a singular teen and have expressed my ideas from both a male and a female perspective. Though I can't present a scenario for every situation parents may encounter, I trust you will find hope and encouragement for your personal parenting journey.

## What Success Looks Like

What does it look like to raise successful teens? Your goal isn't to have a perfect teen. Instead, it is to be a guide toward truth as she navigates an ever-changing world. I want my daughters to live in obedience to the standards set in Scripture. I want them to know the difference between right and wrong and choose to do what honors God. I want them to become everything they desire and everything God desires for them.

Jesus said in Matthew 22:37 that the greatest commandment is "Love the Lord your God with all your heart, all your soul, and all your mind" (NCV). So as it relates to success for my kids and yours, shouldn't our goal be to raise children who, above all, aspire to love Jesus Christ with every facet of their lives? Pause now to pray with me for yourself and your family:

*Father, I thank You for my family. I also thank You for the call You have placed on my life to be the parent my child needs at this moment. I know You have a special plan for my teen and for me in this journey. Please guide me as I work to be the parent You already know I can be. I am thankful that You are here with me every step of the way. Amen.*

# God Matched You with Your Child

Years ago a father and mother were forced to abandon their child. They were convinced it would be the only way to protect their son's life from a ruthless dictator. At first they kept their baby nearby. But after three months they placed him in a small watertight vessel and set him afloat in a river. You can read the story in Exodus 2:1–10:

> A man of the tribe of Levi married a Levite woman, and she became pregnant and gave birth to a son. When she saw that he was a fine child, she hid him for three months. But when she could hide him no longer, she got a papyrus basket for him and coated it with tar and pitch. Then she placed the child in it and put it among the reeds along the bank of the Nile. His sister stood at a distance to see what would happen to him.
>
> Then Pharaoh's daughter went down to the Nile to bathe, and her attendants were walking along the riverbank. She saw the basket among the reeds and sent her female slave to get it. She opened it and saw the baby. He was crying, and she felt sorry for him. "This is one of the Hebrew babies," she said.
>
> Then his sister asked Pharaoh's daughter, "Shall I go and get one of the Hebrew women to nurse the baby for you?"

"Yes, go," she answered. So the girl went and got the baby's mother. Pharaoh's daughter said to her, "Take this baby and nurse him for me, and I will pay you." So the woman took the baby and nursed him. When the child grew older, she took him to Pharaoh's daughter and he became her son. She named him Moses, saying, "I drew him out of the water."

We don't know much about Moses's Egyptian stepmother. We don't even know her name. But we do know she was fearless. She violated a pronouncement of her father, a murderous tyrant who had ordered the execution of every Hebrew-born male (see Exodus 1:8–16). Moses's stepmother knew the risk involved in bringing a Hebrew infant into the palace to live, but she did it anyway.

It wasn't as if Pharaoh's daughter came home and said, "Dad, I accidentally ran a chariot into the side of one of your pyramids." No, she came home knowing full well that Dad hated the Hebrews and wanted their baby sons dead. Then she introduced Dad the tyrant to his newest step-grandson, a Hebrew.

Did it just so happen that on the same day Moses's parents placed him in the Nile River, he was found by someone who had the power and resources to protect him? Is it a fluke that the one who found a baby boy and chose to keep him was the daughter of the dictator who ordered the murder of all Hebrew male babies? There is nothing coincidental about this story. God chose the daughter of Pharaoh, the most powerful man on the planet, to be the stepmother of a son. The son, a Hebrew, would do great things for God and eventually lead His people out of the land of the Egyptian king.

Pharaoh's daughter seemingly is one of the most important people in the Old Testament. Though she isn't known for ascending to the throne, she forever will be known as one chosen by God to fulfill a critical role.

She was the daughter of an Egyptian king, and she became a mother to Moses. God chose her for this purpose.

Likewise, God could have chosen anyone to be the parent of your teen. But He didn't choose just anyone; he chose you. This is no coincidence. No other parent is capable of doing the job He created you to do.

If anyone else had rescued Moses, he would not have received the type of education and upbringing he needed to fulfill the call God placed on his life. The same is true for your teen. The unique plan God has for your child is founded on the reality that God chose you to be his parent. Even before your teen drew a breath, God was preparing you to be the parent to lead him every step of the way.

## Growing Up Is Inevitable

Words can't describe the joy I felt as I stood in the delivery room holding Bailey, our first daughter. It was instant love. A nurse showed up to take Bailey to the hospital nursery for her first nap outside the womb. I walked to the nursery, where, gazing through the window with tear-blurred eyes, I watched my daughter sleep.

I repeated much the same experience two years later with the birth of our second daughter, Brynnan. After each of our daughters was born, I wanted to take her into my arms and never let go.

I had visions of being Super Dad, never messing up, doing everything I could to ensure they would have perfect lives. I took a deep breath and said, "I'm a dad. We'll have so much fun!" And almost as quickly I thought, *I'm a dad. Help!*

Do you remember the hopes and dreams you had for your baby? Do you remember *your* instant love? It's no wonder God describes Himself as our "Everlasting Father" (Isaiah 9:6). There is no love on earth that is more unconditional than that of parents for their children.

Yet change happens fast for our kids. One minute they rely on us for everything. Then, in a blink, they are heading off to prom. Whatever the age of your teen, she faces a world that is always changing. And not only is the world constantly changing, but so is your kid.

Greg, a father of two sons, told me, "My boys are entering the teen years, and I'll admit that I'm uneasy. I remember the things I struggled with and the thoughts I had as a middle school boy. I can't believe I have two boys who are going to be dealing with similar challenges. And I'm not sure I'm prepared to help lead them through it all." Can you relate? I've counseled countless parents who feel the same.

Growing up is inevitable. It is your teen's God-given path to becoming the person he was created to be. Your child is exploring who he is and what really matters most. However, your teen was not created to set out alone on the journey to adulthood. He needs you. But Satan wants your teen (and you) to believe otherwise. He works overtime to convince you *and* your teenager that a strong parent-child relationship is no longer necessary. In the chapters that follow, I'll show you how to combat his lies.

## Your Influence as a Parent

For over twenty-five years I have spoken in front of more than four million people in churches, schools, detention centers, conferences, music festivals, and other venues. I have had numerous conversations with tweens, teens, and college students on almost every topic imaginable. We talk about God, eternity, heaven, hell, social media, sex, pornography, cutting, addictions, divorce, homosexuality, friendships, dating, witnessing, college, and more.

I also have had many conversations with pastors, parents, school administrators, law-enforcement officials, and social workers who ask about teen culture. Though their questions vary and many of the people asking aren't people of faith, I can summarize their questions as "How do we protect our kids from the onslaught of lies they hear as we guide them in making the choices that will influence the rest of their lives?"

My answer in every instance is "Mom and Dad!" Of course, not all kids are growing up in a two-parent family. I meet single-parent moms and dads all the time. If you are a single parent, thanks for reading! You're pulling double duty often, and I know there are days this can be challenging. You've been given the unique privilege of being the parent who is involved daily with your child, and I am cheering for you as you read. Your situation is not a surprise to God, and He is in it with you every step of the way.

I can say that parents are the answer every time because it's true and because I'm a parent too. I see firsthand the influence I have over my daughters as they learn to live by watching how my wife and I live. Bailey and Brynnan watch my life more than they realize.

Even the angry, dismissive, disrespectful teenagers are busy developing their worldviews on life, God, love, sex, friends, money, church, politics, marriage, and entertainment. Much of what they look to for direction is what they see in their parents' lives.

Parents are given a task that is the hardest and most rewarding of all. God didn't haphazardly choose you and me for this job. Bailey and Brynnan are my kids because God chose Amy and me to be the earthly parents to *His* children. Bailey and Brynnan are gifts from God. The same is true for you and your children. "Children are a gift from the Lord; babies are a reward" (Psalm 127:3, NCV).

Satan knows that God has big stuff in store for your teen, and Satan will do everything he can to crash the party. It is critical that you understand that Satan hates your teen. No matter what stands out about him—star athlete, honor-roll student, musician, volunteer working with the homeless—Satan hates your child because he doesn't want God to win.

Who gave Pharaoh the idea in 1526 BC to kill all the Hebrew boys? Satan knew what God had promised Abraham: "To your descendants I give this land, from the Wadi of Egypt to the great river, the Euphrates—the land of the Kenites, Kenizzites, Kadmonites, Hittites, Perrizzites, Rephaites, Amorites, Canaanites, Girgashites and Jebusites" (Genesis 15:18–21). Satan also knew what God had promised Abraham's son Isaac: "Stay in this land for a while, and I will be with you and will bless you. For to you and your descendants I will give all these lands and will confirm the oath I swore to your father Abraham" (26:3).

And Satan knew exactly what God had promised Abraham's grandson Jacob: "I am the LORD, the God of your father Abraham and the God of Isaac. I will give you and your descendants the land on which you are lying" (28:13). Satan knew that God was working toward something big, and he wanted to do everything he could to stop God's plan. He continues to work against God's plan and promise. If anything, he has upped his game.

Why do you think so many teens feel the pressure to give it all away sexually, even when so many parents raise them to live otherwise? Who do you think is behind every tear that runs down the faces of teen girls who fall for these lies?

- "You'll never be as pretty as she is."
- "You're so fat. No one will ever love you looking like that!"
- "If you don't go all the way with him, he's going to move on to someone who will."

And what about the lies that tear down the confidence, self-image, and faith of teenage boys?

- "Porn is no big deal. Everyone's looking at it, but no one talks about it. So keep quiet."
- "You'll never get accepted to college with your grades. You better look for a way to cheat without getting caught or you'll never make the grade."
- "Just drop a little of that into your date's drink and she won't remember anything that happens tonight."

Maybe your teen hasn't fallen for such lies. Or maybe she has. Most likely, you don't know. But no matter how the situation appears to you, your teen is only one choice away from hurt, addiction, and heartbreak.

When a young person tells me about his worst fears and mounting failures, I usually can connect the dots backward from that teen's hurt to his home. Teens ask questions such as "Why is my mom too busy to spend time with me?" or "Why does my dad spend more time with my brother than with me?" I have cried along with many girls and boys who can't understand why their parents don't communicate with them.

It would be foolish of me to tell you, "Be a good parent and all will be well with your child." We know that's not the secret to success. It would be equally foolish for me to ignore all I have learned from listening to teens who long for help, hope, and hugs from a parent. Teens wonder why their parents choose instead to check out.

## My Aha Moment as a Dad

When someone gives you a gift, what is your immediate response?

"I'd really rather have been given something else."

"This is going straight to the regift pile!"

"I hope there's a gift receipt here somewhere."

What *should* be your immediate response? My mama taught me to say thank you no matter how I felt about the gift. As I mentioned earlier, Psalm 127:3 insists that "children are a gift from the LORD; they are a reward from him" (NLT). With that truth in mind, my response to God will always be "Thank You for my children."

How do you parent as a thankful mom or dad? Ask God, "How can I honor You as I parent my teen?" Imagine if every parent paused to ask God's direction on *all* things involved in parenting. What if each of us asked questions such as these:

- "How can I honor God by what our family watches on television and in movies?"
- "How can I honor God by what I teach my teen about sex, love, and dating?"
- "How can I honor God by teaching appropriate use of cell phones?"
- "How can I honor God by ensuring my family is in the Word consistently?"
- "How can I honor God by what I teach my teen about music, the world, evangelism, politics, friendships, helping the poor, finances, and choosing a career?"

In the following chapters, we will look at practical wisdom and approaches to these issues and more.

## This Book Is for You

Maybe you think your teen appears to be doing well, so you aren't sure why you should read a book about parenting. Or maybe the choices she has made so far have left your family at the breaking point. You feel hopeless, ready to throw in the towel. Wherever your teen is at the moment, this book is for you.

First, it's irrelevant whether your teen is in a good or bad place right now. Satan hates young people who are conscientious, responsible, and compassionate just as much as he hates teens who are bullies, refuse to accept responsibility, and remain on probation after breaking the law. He doesn't base his disdain for your child on whether he makes the honor roll or does meth. Satan wants every teen, including *your* teen, to fail.

Second, no matter how it looks on the surface, every teen is trying to answer questions such as "Who am I?"; "What am I going to do with my life?"; and "Who will give me the answers I need about life, love, college, finances, sex, and gender identity?" Every teen has to consider our culture's fluid definitions of right and wrong. The disregard for moral absolutes and the roller-coaster definitions of truth and falsehood create a toxic environment through which your teen must find her way mentally and spiritually.

Third, social media is ever present. Snapchat and Instagram are a way of life for most teens. Posting to Snapchat is the first thing they do in the morning and often the last thing in the evening—like a ritual of life. Cell phones are vital appendages. Social media platforms rule the world, in part because they cater to our increasingly brief attention spans.

Social media, along with all other forms of media, delivers a constant flow of images, video, and content that is of questionable value. A mom told me that her son found himself in the middle of a social media nightmare via Snapchat. After meeting a girl at a party, the mom's teenage son "friended" the girl. What began as an innocent streak (that's Snapchat lingo for a photo conversation between two people) eventually spiraled out of control a few months later. It ended with the issuance of a restraining order against the girl to protect the boy from a neurotic, self-destructive girl looking for attention and willing to do just about anything to feel secure.

Social media has changed the way the world communicates. It demands that you, as a parent, understand how it is shaping your teen—

and you! In a later chapter we'll consider practical tips on how to keep your family safe.

Last, your teen wants and needs an involved, engaged, all-in parent. Numerous conversations with teens who speak with me at my events begin with heart-wrenching statements such as these:

- "My dad lives at home, but he really 'left' us years ago."
- "I never read the Bible with members of my family, much less pray with them."
- "I can't remember the last time my mom told me 'I love you.'"
- "We never eat dinner together as a family unless we are watching Netflix."
- "I wish my parents would let me talk about what's really going on. They never seem to listen, but they're good at screaming."
- "I'm pretty sure my parents wouldn't care if I just disappeared forever."

Teens tell me, even when their words may not say it, "I need Mom and Dad in it with me every day." The fact that you are reading this book indicates you have big dreams for your teen and want to be the parent he needs. Although we often don't know what our kids are thinking or feeling, we are called to dream big, pray like mad, and never give up hope.

## Commitment Time

I'd like to ask you to make a commitment to stay the course and not get frustrated as we talk about life, God, culture, and parenting as they relate to your son or daughter. On the following pages, you will likely read some things you will not want to believe. It is also possible you will read some things you won't think you need to believe. But I guarantee that everything I write in this book is critical for you as a parent. In addition, your teen is counting on your commitment to stick it out and have patience. Here are three critical commitments you need to make.

### 1. I'm all in!

Maybe you are thinking, *This book isn't for me. My teen is doing great! She's plugged in at church, goes to summer camp, and is excelling at school.* Or maybe you are at the other end of the spectrum. Your teen is about to graduate. She has made choices that have pushed your family to the brink. You are feeling hopeless, ready to give up on it all.

Wherever your teen is on her journey, this book is for you. Your child needs you to be all in. You have a lot to look forward to and get ready for, and it's never too soon or too late to be all in.

### 2. I'm all ears!

No matter what it looks like on the surface, every teen struggles with temptations, fears, and challenges. Every teen has to navigate the confusing waters of today's culture. It's important you realize this before moving forward.

Even a Jesus-loving, church-attending teen who is a straight-A student will deal with extreme challenges during the journey from child to adult. Remember, Satan doesn't care if your teen is on the honor roll. No matter his grades, talent, or looks, the devil hates him.

I'm going to challenge you to implement some steps that, at the moment, may seem unnecessary or unrealistic. But I urge you to resist the desire to move quickly past these topics and instead take these issues to God, asking Him to reveal what He would have you hear and implement as it pertains to your son or daughter. Proverbs 1:5 says, "Let the wise listen and add to their learning, and let the discerning get guidance." As you read this book, make it your prayer to listen to what God would have you hear, and then do what He would have you do.

### 3. I'm all His!

Just because you read this book and apply its advice does not mean that your child will choose to embrace a God-focused life. No matter how hard you work at being the best mom or dad, your teen is a human being with free will. She can and will mess it all up—more than once.

You and I need all the help we can get. Parenting is tough. We need God at the center of our lives. I want to challenge you to surrender your will, your wants, your theories, and your priorities to God every day. Ask Him (and mean it) to lead every area of your life. Remember, God could have chosen anyone to be the parent of your teen. But He didn't choose just anyone; He chose you!

# Reality Is Hard, but You Have the Advantage

It is a beautiful day in paradise. *Every* day is a beautiful day in paradise. The trees are tall and lush; they are filled with beautiful varieties of flowers and fruit. Everywhere you look you see perfection—in the air, in the water, and on the land. Animals of all types move freely. Surely there is no place on earth more perfect than this.

God created Adam and Eve to live in the Garden of Eden. Their Father gave them everything they could want or need. They had no worries and no fears. They had perfect lives. But all this was about to change forever.

The serpent was more crafty than any other beast of the field that the LORD God had made.

He said to the woman, "Did God actually say, 'You shall not eat of any tree in the garden'?" And the woman said to the serpent, "We may eat of the fruit of the trees in the garden, but God said, 'You shall not eat of the fruit of the tree that is in the midst of the garden, neither shall you touch it, lest you die.'" But the serpent said to the woman, "You will not surely die. For

God knows that when you eat of it your eyes will be opened, and you will be like God, knowing good and evil." So when the woman saw that the tree was good for food, and that it was a delight to the eyes, and that the tree was to be desired to make one wise, she took of its fruit and ate, and she also gave some to her husband who was with her, and he ate. Then the eyes of both were opened, and they knew that they were naked. And they sewed fig leaves together and made themselves loincloths. (Genesis 3:1–7, ESV)

Satan lied to God's first earthly children. He convinced them that their Father was wrong and that following God's lead would never satisfy them. Satan said all the wrong things in all the right ways in order to get Adam and Eve to look past what God said and see things from Satan's point of view. Look again at some of the ways Eve's perspective shifted following her conversation with Satan: "The woman saw that the tree was good for food, and that it was a delight to the eyes, and that the tree was to be desired to make one wise" (verse 6, ESV). This most likely wasn't the first time Eve had seen the fruit in question, but after her fateful exchange with Satan, it most likely *was* the first time she had seen it as delightful and desirable. In one brief conversation Satan connected with Eve in an intimate way. Then she saw everything differently. Satan deceived her into taking a bite, and this would affect every daughter and son who would walk the planet from that moment forward.

It makes me mad that Adam and Eve allowed Satan to distort their perspective on God and reality. And I'm sad because the serpent who deceived Adam and Eve is the same serpent who continues to deceive all God's children.

Though Adam and Eve were adults, their story is the first proof the Bible offers us of how much Satan hates us—and our kids. At the beginning of time on earth, he went right to work to deceive God's first humans. In order for us to understand how Satan operates, let's review five things we know about him:

1. **Satan is an angel who rebelled against God.** The Enemy was tossed out of heaven following his rebellion:

> How you are fallen from heaven,
>> O Day Star, son of Dawn!
> How you are cut down to the ground,
>> you who laid the nations low!
> You said in your heart,
>> "I will ascend to heaven;
> above the stars of God
>> I will set my throne on high;
> I will sit on the mount of assembly
>> in the far reaches of the north;
> I will ascend above the heights of the clouds;
>> I will make myself like the Most High."
> But you are brought down to Sheol,
>> to the far reaches of the pit. (Isaiah 14:12–15, ESV)

2. **His name means "the adversary."** He is a schemer who is extremely skilled at deception: "Even Satan changes himself to look like an angel of light" (2 Corinthians 11:14, NCV).

3. **His plan always opposes God's plan.** "Put on the full armor of God, so that you can take your stand against the devil's schemes" (Ephesians 6:11).

4. **He is a tempter who is setting a trap.** "The tempter came to him and said, 'If you are the Son of God, tell these stones to become bread'" (Matthew 4:3).

5. **He rules this world.** "Now is the judgment of this world; now
   will the ruler of this world be cast out" (John 12:31, ESV).

For a time, God is allowing Satan to conduct his evil work. He
knows that his days are numbered and that his deception will end at the
gates of hell (see John 12:31). Until the final day of his rule over the earth,
he will work like mad to fulfill two goals. First, he wants to take people,
including your kid, to hell. Jesus warned us of this in John 10:10: "The
thief comes only to steal and kill and destroy." Jesus didn't mention hell
by name in this passage, but if you look at the Greek words that are translated here as *steal, kill,* and *destroy,* you will understand their tragic
nature.

The word *steal* comes from the Greek word *kléptēs,* which means "a
false teacher, who does not care to instruct men, but abuses their confidence for their own gain."[1] Satan will do whatever he deems necessary to
steal your child's confidence for his own gain. This is what he is good at
doing. The Enemy works to confuse young people in the hope that he can
deceive them into believing inaccurate or untrue things. Why? So he can
destroy lives. Danielle, a sixteen-year-old I met in California, told me,
"I've struggled with self-worth for many years. I have an eating disorder,
and I can't stop obsessing about my appearance. I make myself throw up
all the time because I have to maintain my weight."

Danielle said many of her friends consider her a beautiful girl. She
was elected to her high school's homecoming court two years in a row. I
wonder what her friends would think if they knew the real Danielle, the
girl who vomits because she has zero self-confidence and self-worth. She
is one example of the many teens Satan has deceived with the lie "You are
worthless!"

The words *to kill* come from the Greek word *thuo,* which means "to
sacrifice."[2] Satan is sacrificing something short term for a greater payoff in

the long term. Satan does not want us to enjoy anything. He hates our joy. But he may be willing to offer us momentary pleasure in return for our long-standing misery.

Isn't this what Satan offered to Eve? He was willing to give her a momentary bite of something delightful and desirable because he knew the end result would be her separation from God. In the same way, Satan knows if he can entice your teen with a bite of the world's delightful and desirable options, he has a good chance of hardening her heart to God.

We see proof of this with the third important word Jesus uses in this passage. The word translated in English as *destroy* in the Greek means "to be completely ruined." Satan wants to completely ruin your teen, not just in this life but also for eternity. He wants to lure teenagers into embracing everything that goes against God's will and purpose, trying to make sure they never choose to receive Jesus Christ as Lord. If Satan wins, he cashes in forever. His prize is your kid's soul.

Your teen may already have given his heart to Jesus. If so, it could be easy to believe that you can ease up on your vigilance. Don't buy this lie. Remember, Satan's second goal is to relentlessly deceive teens in order to keep them from becoming the people God wants them to become. In Genesis 3:1 the Bible introduces Satan as being crafty. Since the moment of his first deception on earth, he has been creating snares for us all.

How does this information help you and me become better parents? Satan helps guide and shape cultural trends. Your teen lives in a very different world from the one you recall. Each generation experiments as it tests and challenges issues such as truth, God, sexuality, and morality. In that respect, today's generation is no different. But the world changes with time, and as the world changes, Satan's traps change. Satan tries to ensure that culture shapes your teen in ways that you, and God's Word, never can.

## Ten Ways Today's Teens Think About Culture

To the young people in Generation Z, the influence and effects of popular culture are invisible. To them, the culture is like oxygen. It always has been there, and everyone they know largely follows the beat of what surrounds them. They don't operate according to the rules of logic that you are familiar with. As you consider these paradigms of thought and belief, think creatively about ways your family can discuss these issues.

### 1. Social media reigns!

Your teen's unending digital conversation consists of four steps: phone in hand, engage the phone's camera, strike a pose, and send. A digital image of something or someone is on its way to someone else. Or in the case of a post on social media, it's on its way to a *lot* of people. The top social media app for Generation Z is Snapchat. More than eight in ten teens use it.[3] Other apps are WhatsApp, Telegram, Kik, WeChat, and ASKfm.

The hot app today might fall into disuse by week's end, but social media is here to stay. I recently asked a group of teens, "On average, how many snaps do you send each day?" Every one of them said more than two hundred. What does this obsession say about what teens think of themselves? They fear being overlooked; they crave attention; they overdo things in an attempt to fit in. One teen explained, "When I am sitting at home on the weekend and I see many of my friends snapping and tweeting, it makes me feel like I'm missing out on all the fun. It also makes me feel 'less than' because I'm not doing whatever it is they are doing. When I do snap or tweet, I feel like I am saying to the world, 'Look at me! My life is important too!'"

Presently, the one social media metric by which teens live and die is the snap streak. You probably know that a Snapchat streak is when you send direct snaps back and forth with someone for consecutive days. The longer teens go without missing a day, the longer the streak. Snapchat uses emojis to reward users who have long streaks. Teens have shared with me their devastation over losing a streak.

Sadly, many teens view streaks as the default measure of success. Teens feel more popular and often have a greater sense of self-worth when they have indications of being socially accepted. Long-term streaks validate their social success. One high school junior explained it in these words: "When I see others having a lot of streaks, I view those people as popular and think, *Man, I've got to have that too.*" Another high school student told me, "I even wake up early on school days just so I can keep my streaks alive." What does all this tell us about where our teens obtain their sense of significance and self-worth?

## 2. It's all about me.

Social media and self-obsession go hand in hand. Teenagers—both girls and boys—are obsessed with their images. Having traveled for more than two decades talking with teenagers, I can tell you the one obsession that is front and center with teen guys: having the perfect body! There always have been teen boys who have worked out to stay in shape. However, I've never seen it become the obsession it is today. Why? It's connected to this generation's belief that "it's all about me." Teen boys see other teen boys who obviously have spent time in the gym getting their posts and snaps reposted by girls they don't even know. Do you get the connection? Boys get the body in hopes of getting the repost, and thus they can feel better about themselves.

You probably have watched your teen stop everything in order to concentrate on capturing the perfect angle for a flawless selfie. Mobile devices with vastly improved cameras have changed how teens perceive themselves. The easy ability to take better-quality photos has elevated their levels of concern over how others perceive them. My daughter

Brynnan explained that everyone wants to be in the "one-hundred-likes club." This refers to attaining a minimum of one hundred likes with each Instagram post. Here's what's alarming: selfies aren't merely snapshots of how our teens are living; they are demonstrations of teens' obsession with getting the perfect selfie, which has *changed* how they live.

For some teens it may be less about social media, snaps, and selfies and more about something equally important to them in their state of self-obsession. I recently prayed with a locker room full of high school football players before they took the field. Gabe, a wide receiver, explained his and his teammates' obsession with having perfect bodies. "All of us guys are completely consumed with our bodies. We see NFL players who are cut and are amazing athletes. We all want to have amazing bodies. I guess you could say it's our obsession."

Whether it involves selfies, a perfect body, money, the right clothes, the latest gadget, or a jacked-up truck, this generation has grown up embracing the slogan "I have to have the best, be the best, and look the best." Almost every teen knows other teens who have posted pictures or videos of themselves on YouTube or social media and experienced some level of overnight popularity as a result. Many of the Gen Z teens I meet are dreaming of the day when the same happens for them.

### 3. I have to be better looking.
It's no secret that the fashion industry manipulates how models look in photos, thus promoting unrealistic body image and false conceptions of physical beauty. The practice feeds efforts to achieve unachievable body stereotypes.

Amy and I activated an opt-in feature on Facebook that requires our approval before anyone can tag either one of us in a posted photo. This eliminates the dreaded "I can't believe you posted *that* picture of me!" Instagram takes the opt-in feature to new heights (or lows, depending on your perspective). Users can choose from apps that help them disguise, hide, shed, and fix just about anything they don't like in a picture of themselves. PhotoWonder, which has more than a hundred million users, has "slimify" and "blemish fix" options. The PicMonkey app can whiten your teeth and give you a spray tan. All of this alerts me to the reality that I have to work hard to remind my daughters that their value, beauty, and significance aren't defined by how many likes they amass or how well they develop their glamorizing skills while doctoring a photo.

Satan is winning in this arena. In what appears to be merely innocent tweets, posts, and snaps, the Enemy is working to instill in young people the idea of "It's my life, and I can live as I please and post as I live."

Obviously, Jesus never commented specifically on social media, but He knew the effect it would have on this generation. John the Baptist—who was attracting crowds with his preaching, baptizing, and proclamation of the coming Messiah—pointed out that his own fame was not the goal. John said, "[Jesus] must increase, but I must decrease" (John 3:30, NKJV). In order for our teens to honor God with their lives, they must be less concerned with themselves and far more focused on God's plan and purpose for them.

Satan wants the opposite. As your teen becomes more self-absorbed, Satan wants her to grow less and less spiritually engaged with Jesus Christ.

## 4. I will decide what is right and wrong.

In John 8:44 Jesus said about Satan, "He was a murderer from the beginning, not holding to the truth, for there is no truth in him. When he lies, he speaks his native language, for he is a liar and the father of lies." There is overwhelming evidence that Satan has succeeded in lying to this generation via pop culture—convincing teens that right and wrong are personal decisions, not absolutes. They have been assured that morals and ethics are dictated not by God but by personal preference. A high school senior told me, "It's less about what is right and more about what moves me. I often base my decision-making on how a situation makes me feel rather than on what is right."

Culture is rewriting the definition of right and wrong. Teenagers believe it is okay to do anything you want, any way you want to, as long as it works for you in the moment. If you want proof of this, ask a group of teens to discuss ethical and moral issues such as euthanasia, suicide, gay marriage, abortion, sin, and religious tolerance. You will most likely see that teens, even many who are Christians, hold varying beliefs about the moral and ethical absolutes.

At a conference I explained these ideas and then asked, "How many of you believe there is absolute truth?" In an audience of more than twelve hundred teens, only about one hundred raised their hands. Fewer than 9 percent of the students at this Christian conference believed that important life issues could be considered either absolutely right or absolutely wrong.

### 5. Sin is just another thing I do.

I was asked to speak every week for a year in chapel at my daughter's Christian school. I decided to begin the school year by having the students complete a survey. The survey asked questions about God, the Bible, personal struggles, and habits. I don't remember every comment, but I haven't forgotten one from a senior girl who wrote, "I've been looking at porn for so long that I don't even consider it a struggle anymore. It's become such a normal part of my life that it just is what it is: another thing I do."

A college sophomore working as a counselor at a camp where I spoke told me, "I really don't see a big difference in the way my Christian and non-Christian friends live. We kind of all do the same stuff, good and bad, and no one really blinks an eye."

The writer of Psalm 81:12 wrote, "I [God] gave them over to their stubborn hearts to follow their own devices." Paul wrote a similar warning in Romans 1:24: "God gave them over in the sinful desires of their hearts." The Enemy has deceived many of our teens into believing that sin is no big deal. But it's a huge deal, and your teen counts on you to help him never become callous and casual with sin.

### 6. Let's change the world!

Generation Z wants to make the world a better place. They want to be engaged in movements that promote change and empower people and communities to thrive. They believe in social justice and have little tolerance for those who don't.

I meet teens everywhere who are concerned about the environment, freeing young girls from the sex-slave trade, providing clean drinking water to those in need, feeding the poor, and more. They share with me their stories of hope for a better world. It is rare that I speak at a church that doesn't already have some type of student-driven "Let's change the world" campaign. For many years youth groups have taken trips to other countries to do good work. Today almost every teen and youth pastor I meet wants to take such a trip. This is one of the most popular outreaches among youth groups—taking a mission trip to another country. Gen Z teens post and tweet about ideas, concerns, and causes important to them and the world. You have a tremendous opportunity to help mold the aspirations of your teen in a way that teaches her not only to do good in the world but also to point the world to Jesus Christ.

Even in this realm, the Enemy will work to convince your teen that meeting the world's economic, social, political, and humanitarian needs is good enough. But it's not. Providing clean drinking water in an undeveloped country; creating sustainable energy using wind, solar power, or water; or working to feed malnourished children can distract teens from engaging in the most important humanitarian need of all: salvation through Jesus Christ. Satan is an expert at getting us busy with things that are really good while distracting us from the thing that is the best.

One of the greatest attributes of this generation of teens is their desire to make the world better. We need to help our kids see that through humanitarian efforts there is an even greater evangelistic opportunity. Jesus said in Matthew 28:18–20, "All authority in heaven and on earth has been given to me. Therefore go and make disciples of all nations, baptizing them in the name of the Father and of the Son and of the Holy Spirit, and teaching them to obey everything I have commanded you. And surely I am with you always, to the very end of the age."

### 7. I'm not sure I believe that the Bible is completely true.

Teens are extremely spiritual. But although many believe in God, their beliefs about Him often are defined by the culture, not the Bible. In *The Jesus Survey,* more than eight hundred teenagers attending Christian summer camps were asked about God, heaven, the Bible, and Jesus. Eighty-six percent said they believe that the Bible is somewhat trustworthy; seven in ten doubted that what the Bible says about Jesus is true.[4]

These numbers reflect the beliefs of students who claim to be Christ followers. In saying they don't believe fully in the Bible or in who Jesus claims to be, these Christian teens are contradicting their faith. Such a revelation should alarm you. It alarms me.

Who or what is to blame for this generation's lack of faith in the Bible? Satan, of course. The culture, absolutely. The church, probably. Parents, most definitely. After more than twenty-five years spent working with teens, I can say with confidence that parents don't care enough to make sure their kids believe what is true about the Bible. Rather than debate with yourself the degree to which the statement applies to you, instead consider these questions:

- How often is your family reading or studying the Bible together?
- When was the last time your family had a spiritual discussion about the authenticity of the Bible?
- Are you praying every day that God's Spirit will protect your family, specifically your teen, from the onslaught of Satan's lies?
- What is your strategy for prioritizing the Word of God in your family? How can it be improved?

It is imperative before you move forward that you understand how serious Satan is about lying to your teen. He wants nothing more than for him to believe that what the Bible says about creation, God, Jesus, the cross, heaven, and hell is a lie. He knows that if he can get your teen to doubt the reliable truth of Scripture, he has a good chance of getting him to walk away from his faith.

## 8. Straight or gay is okay.

When I was a college freshman, one of my professors was a lesbian who was willing to discuss her lifestyle choice in the classroom. Almost undoubtedly, your teen knows someone who is gay, lesbian, bisexual, or transgender. Both of my daughters are close to two of our neighbors who are lesbians. We discussed with our daughters the need to love everyone as Christ does without loving everyone's choices.

Many teens consider the LGBTQ movement to be cool. A leader at a Christian camp told me, "It really doesn't matter whether you are gay or straight. As long as you love Jesus and have received him as your savior, then it's all good." This is coming from a Christian counselor who speaks into the lives of teens. As you know, Generation Z is growing up in a culture that embraces same-sex relationships and transgenderism. Saying that these things are wrong can make you seem intolerant.

I believe that this issue is going to be the single most divisive issue in the church and among Christians. In 2015 the United States Supreme Court declared gay marriage legal nationwide.[5] Most teens I meet know someone who is in a same-sex relationship, and they're okay with the LGBTQ lifestyle.

## 9. Porn is the norm.

"My first exposure to porn was in eighth grade. I was on my phone and accidentally saw pictures of naked girls. I felt guilty. But a few days later, I went looking again. This time it wasn't an accident." This is the story of Jacob, age seventeen.

Most teens I counsel tell me they have viewed porn. This is why studies such as the one conducted by the University of New Hampshire should be of little surprise. The study found that 93 percent of male college students and 62 percent of female college students had seen online porn before they were eighteen.[6] More than two out of five young people age ten to seventeen who use the internet say they've seen online pornography in the past year.[7]

The University of Indiana surveyed more than six hundred teens and their parents. The results revealed the naivete of many parents. Twice as many of these teens had watched porn as what the parents believed.[8] To many teens, porn is the norm. It's accessible. It's free. And it's merely a click away.

## 10. Sex is no big deal.

Because so many teens are checking out porn, it should be no surprise that many also experiment sexually. A high school student told me, "Having sex with my boyfriend isn't that big of a deal. I've dated several guys since the eighth grade, and I've had sex with all of them. The first time I had sex I was really scared. But now it's a way of bringing me closer to the one I love. For me and my friends, sex is just something we do to express how we feel about someone."

Exposure to pornography skews perceptions about what constitutes a healthy relationship. To many teens, porn and sex are as routine as anything else in their busy lives. And Satan works overtime to convince them that anyone who believes otherwise is out of touch with reality.

## There Is Still Hope

You may feel burdened about the state of today's teens and how your teen fits into all this. I find great comfort in the words of the Hebrew prophet Jeremiah: "'I know the plans I have for you,' declares the LORD, 'plans to prosper you and not to harm you, plans to give you hope and a future'" (Jeremiah 29:11). No matter how maddening the world is, God is still in control. He wants to bless your teen with an abundant life and remind you that you are the one He chose to help convey this truth to her.

What is the key to inheriting this promise? The answer is found in the next two verses: "Then you will call on me and come and pray to me, and I will listen to you. You will seek me and find me when you seek me with all your heart" (verses 12–13). The key words for you and everyone in your family are *all your heart*. We find hope when we choose to seek God wholeheartedly.

Satan knows that if he can prevent your teen from pursuing a committed relationship with Jesus Christ, he likely has gained a soul. Satan knows the good plans God has for your teen, and he schemes to release all hell on earth to keep him from becoming everything God promises.

But Scripture tells us, "You, dear children, are from God and have overcome them, because the one who is in you is greater than the one who is in the world" (1 John 4:4). Although Satan is out to end it all for my kids and yours, we have One on our side who is greater than any lie from Satan. What we have to do is continue to help our kids identify the lies coming from the Enemy. No matter how hard Satan works to deceive, we, too, must work hard to empower our teenagers to understand the errors of this culture.

# Five Questions Your Teen Needs to Answer

The Bible tells us that after Moses died, God spoke to Joshua:

Moses My servant is dead. Now you and all the people prepare to cross over the Jordan to the land I am giving the Israelites. I have given you every place where the sole of your foot treads, just as I promised Moses. Your territory will be from the wilderness and Lebanon to the great Euphrates River—all the land of the Hittites—and west to the Mediterranean Sea. No one will be able to stand against you as long as you live. I will be with you, just as I was with Moses. I will not leave you or forsake you.

Be strong and courageous, for you will distribute the land I swore to their fathers to give them as an inheritance. Above all, be strong and very courageous to carefully observe the whole instruction My servant Moses commanded you. Do not turn from it to the right or the left, so that you will have success wherever you go. This book of instruction must not depart from your mouth; you are to recite it day and night so that you may carefully observe everything written in it. For then you will prosper and succeed in whatever you do. Haven't I commanded you: be strong and courageous? Do not be afraid or discouraged, for the LORD your God is with you wherever you go. (Joshua 1:2–9, HCSB)

Joshua had been relying on Moses for nearly everything; now Moses was gone. The more than one million Hebrews camping in the wilderness started looking to Joshua for leadership. God commanded Joshua to cross the Jordan River into the Promised Land. Can you imagine such a responsibility?

Most days Amy and I run around like crazy caring for our daughters —packing school lunches; getting the girls to volleyball, soccer, tennis, and basketball practice; and tackling homework and school projects. Then there are piano lessons to drive them to, exams to help them study for, student-council meetings and parties to help organize, laundry to do, water bottles to fill, and did I mention homework? I'm sure your schedule is similarly hectic.

But Joshua was responsible for more than *one million people.* How could he keep an entire nation moving in the right direction? If I were to speculate, I'd say it was by knowing the importance of two words: *above all.*

In the first six verses of Joshua 1, God made clear what He expected. He told Joshua that if he followed God's instructions, "No one will be able to stand against you as long as you live. I will be with you, just as I was with Moses. I will not leave you or forsake you" (verse 5, HCSB). In verse 7 we see the key words *above all.* God's instructions and promises would be worthless unless Joshua obeyed God's Word above all else. Your responsibility as a parent—and mine—is that "this book of instruction must not depart from your mouth." We also read in Deuteronomy,

You will again obey the LORD and follow all his commands I am giving you today. Then the LORD your God will make you most prosperous in all the work of your hands and in the fruit of your womb, the young of your livestock and the crops of your land. The LORD will again delight in you and make you prosperous, just as he delighted in your ancestors, if you obey the LORD your God and keep his commands and decrees that are written in this Book of the Law and turn to the LORD your God with all your heart and with all your soul. (30:8–10)

The takeaway for us as parents isn't that we should recite Scripture to our kids day and night; instead, we need to integrate God's Word into our everyday lives so these truths shape us in ways that are honoring to God. Up to this point, your teen's values and beliefs have been shaped by family, church, relationships, and culture. But what about the powerful, life-changing impact of God's Word?

## How Parents Fail to Instill God's Word

I don't use the word *failure* lightly. There is no other word I can use that describes the lack of biblical confidence parents are instilling in their teens. Parents generally have failed to help their teens know the Word of God and confidently live, *above all,* as God commands them to live. This is the key to our success as families. Answer these questions:

- Does your family have a consistent family devotional time?
- Does your teen have a consistent personal devotional time?

Much of what your teen believes is likely a result of what you have taught her and what she is expected to believe. But you are far from the only influence in your child's life. In middle school and high school, tweens and teens jockey for position and significance among friends and classmates. As they move into new circles of influence, much of what they have believed so far is challenged by a chorus of new voices.

While speaking on a college campus, I met Kristin. She was in her sophomore year, and she mentioned she had undergone a "spiritual shift." She told me, "I was the girl back home who grew up in church, attended all the youth-group events, went on several mission trips, and even consistently sang in the youth worship band." But she explained that since arriving at college, things had changed.

"Once I got here and started making friends," she said, "I realized my beliefs about God weren't as strong as I thought. Church became less of a priority, and sleeping in on Sunday mornings became routine.

"By the end of my freshman year, I wasn't even going to church or really even reading my Bible. I admit that a few friends (and one professor in particular) have really pushed me to question a lot about my faith. I'm not sure where I am with it all right now. I guess you could say I've lost confidence in some of the things I once believed about God and I'm still trying to figure it out."

Such questioning can be an important process for anyone in search of answers about life, God, and salvation. It is important for you, as a parent, to be sensitive to such questions, since they may alert you to signs your child is abandoning his faith. It also is critical that your teen has confidence in what he believes. If teens are not confident in their beliefs, eventually their belief systems will be shaken by the input they receive from someone or by the way circumstances affect them.

## Five Critical Questions for Your Teen

Your teen should be able to clearly defend what she believes. Teens are challenged from all angles. The culture has become increasingly secular and often discriminatory toward religion, Christianity in particular. In light of that, help your teen solidify in her mind the answers to these questions.

### 1. Do I believe the Bible is the absolute truth of God?

I recently had lunch with a good friend, Aaron, who is Brynnan and Bailey's student pastor at our church. I asked, "What is the greatest struggle you have as it relates to reaching Generation Z?" He answered,

> It's the fact that many [teens] do not believe the Bible is the absolute Word of God. . . . Students have to understand that everything about their existence begins with the fact that God is who He says He is and that His Word is proof of it all. If they don't believe this, then it's going to be almost impossible for us as pastors and parents to help them believe that what God says in His Word is true as it relates to eternity, sin, Satan, saving sex until marriage, homosexuality, salvation, and more.

Everything begins here. If your teen doesn't believe that the Bible is the infallible Word of God, then it's only a matter of time before he loses confidence in who God is and what He says about how He desires each of us to live. How your teen responds to the tsunami of information, myths, and lies of the Enemy rests solely on what he believes about the Word of God.

Your teen's ability to answer this question in the affirmative is second only to the question of where she will spend eternity. Of course, the more you are in the Word, the more you will believe in it. Here are a few powerful verses for your family to memorize about the authenticity of Scripture:

Man does not live on bread alone but on every word that comes
from the mouth of the LORD. (Deuteronomy 8:3)

As for God, his way is perfect:
    the LORD's word is flawless;
    he shields all who take refuge in him. (2 Samuel 22:31)

The entirety of Your word is truth,
And every one of Your righteous judgments endures forever.
        (Psalm 119:160, NKJV)

## 2. Do I believe Christianity is distinct from other religions?

At a recent Christian student conference, I outlined some of the core beliefs of Christianity. Then I asked a group of teens what their faith would
be if it were boiled down to one sentence. Here are snippets from some of
the responses:

- "I believe all religions lead to the same God." (Anna,
  fourteen)
- "There's more than one way to heaven." (Carter, fifteen)
- "Sure, Jesus sinned. Everybody sins." (Zoe, sixteen)
- "Hell isn't real. I think hell is just in your mind." (Gabrielle,
  fifteen)
- "Of course I believe in evolution. Doesn't everybody with
  a brain?" (Jordan, seventeen)
- "What's most important is that you treat other people with
  tolerance." (Evan, sixteen)
- "Christianity, Hinduism, Islam, Judaism—everybody prays
  to the same God. It's just that God has different ways he
  (or she) is seen." (Reagan, eighteen)

These responses from Gen Z students reveal that many of them hold strongly to counter-Christian beliefs. Such comments greatly burden me, for I believe that many church-attending teens see Christianity as just one of any number of acceptable religious choices. Jesus talked about the mark of a follower: "Not everyone who says to me, 'Lord, Lord,' will enter the kingdom of heaven, but only the one who does the will of my Father who is in heaven" (Matthew 7:21).

Some religious groups worship false gods. Some believe in God but don't believe that Jesus was His Son. Some think that Jesus was a real person but not that He died for us and was raised from the dead. Some don't believe that the Bible is the infallible Word of God.

Buddhism says there is no God. Instead, Buddhists believe that when you die, you return to being at one with the universe, much like a drop of water blending back into an ocean.

Hinduism claims that there are many gods and that Brahman (the ultimate power underlying the universe) is in everything and in each person. Hindus believe that a person needs only to rediscover his or her inner god in order to reach a state of nirvana (eternal bliss).

Islam does believe in one supreme God: Allah. However, Muslims do not recognize the human plight of original sin. According to Islam, God is not considered a loving "father" and Allah has no son.

Judaism proclaims the one true God. However, with the exception of Messianic Jews who have come to a saving knowledge of Christ, Jews don't believe that Jesus was God's Son. They don't believe He was the Christ who came to earth, lived a sinless life, died for the sins of humanity, rose from the dead three days later, and offers salvation and eternity in heaven to anyone who believes in Him and chooses to receive Him as savior and lord.

In comparison to these world religions, Christianity is unique.

Nothing is more critical than helping your teen believe four truths about the Christian faith:

1. God is the *only* God, and Jesus is the Son of God, who came to earth, died for humanity, and conquered death by coming back to life and proving that He is the one true savior of the world. "Christ also suffered once for sins, the righteous for the unrighteous, that he might bring us to God, being put to death in the flesh but made alive in the spirit" (1 Peter 3:18, ESV).

2. The Bible is God's Word and the ultimate authority for everything we do. "The word of God is alive and active. Sharper than any double-edged sword, it penetrates even to dividing soul and spirit, joints and marrow; it judges the thoughts and attitudes of the heart" (Hebrews 4:12).

3. We follow Jesus Christ. "Whoever serves me must follow me; and where I am, my servant also will be. My Father will honor the one who serves me" (John 12:26).

4. We can't save ourselves. "By grace you have been saved through faith, and that not of yourselves; it is the gift of God" (Ephesians 2:8, NKJV).

### 3. Do I believe there are multiple ways to get to heaven?

Hindus believe in reincarnation based on Karma, which determines what entity they will be born into in their next life. Mormons believe in an afterlife but that before going to heaven, they need to prepare by going to a temporary spirit world. Scientology, Judaism, and Islam each have differing views about heaven.

As Christians, we choose to believe in and live for Jesus. Christians believe that faith in Jesus is the only way to get to heaven. You can't just be a good person or just do good deeds (though, of course, if you believe in Jesus, you will want to do those things). There's only one path to eternal life and it's through Jesus, who said, "I am the way, the truth, and the life. No one comes to the Father except through Me" (John 14:6, NKJV).

### 4. Do I believe that all other religions are false?

In Matthew 7:15 Jesus warned, "Watch out for false prophets. They come to you in sheep's clothing, but inwardly they are ferocious wolves." It will be only a matter of time before a friend, a high school teacher or college professor, an employer, or potentially a future spouse tries to convince your teen that all religious paths lead to heaven. Jesus made it clear in Matthew 7 that such people, even people your teen loves, are hungry wolves. There is only one way to heaven, and it's through a relationship with Jesus Christ.

As you create a spiritual environment that honors God above all else, you will realize that much of the Christian faith is unsettling to the world. Because of the world's standards, you and your teen are likely to be labeled homophobes, xenophobes, misogynists, racists and bigots, closed minded, superstitious, ignorant, and haters.

Amy and I had a powerful conversation with our daughters about this. One of Brynnan's friends sent her a text stating he doesn't believe that Jesus is the only way to heaven. He told Brynnan, "For you to tell me that you are right about this and I am wrong is very narrow minded of you." This text, though difficult for Brynnan to process, gave us a chance to discuss the fact that some people, possibly even those you count as close friends, are going to disagree with you at times. Choosing to believe that the Bible is the ultimate authority means you will be at odds with the world.

When teens choose to stand for such a set of beliefs, they are likely to pay a price. If they do not settle in their hearts that all other religions are false, they eventually will develop the "I'll consider your religion if you consider mine" philosophy.

Just how serious is God about this? Second Corinthians 6:14–17 says,

> Do not be yoked together with unbelievers. For what do righteousness and wickedness have in common? Or what fellowship can light have with darkness? What harmony is there between Christ and Belial? Or what does a believer have in common with an unbeliever? What agreement is there between the temple of God and idols? For we are the temple of the living God. As God has said:
>
> > "I will live with them
> > > and walk among them,
> > and I will be their God,
> > > and they will be my people."
>
> Therefore,
> "Come out from them
> > and be separate,
> > says the Lord."

Once we open our minds to false teaching and then choose to be unequally yoked with someone of another religion (whether it be a friend, girlfriend, boyfriend, or spouse), we open ourselves up to a spirit of deception. Of course, this verse isn't saying that you or anyone in your family should avoid all contact with anyone who believes differently than you do about God. The Bible makes it clear that Jesus spent time with many people who didn't believe. He "came to seek and to save the lost" (Luke 19:10). However, it is important to help our kids understand that a close, deeply committed, intimate relationship with someone who isn't a believer is dangerous.

### 5. Do I believe in the deity of Jesus?

The Bible is clear that Jesus is the Son of God. "In the beginning was the Word, and the Word was with God, and the Word was God. He was in the beginning with God. All things were made through him, and without him was not any thing made that was made. In him was life, and the life was the light of men" (John 1:1–4, ESV).

Jesus was born of a virgin, lived a sinless life, was crucified, died for our sins, rose from the dead, and ascended to heaven to reign at the right hand of God. The world denies this truth, and Satan will work hard to convince your teen it is false. It will be only a matter of time before your teen meets people who say they believe in Jesus but really just believe He was a moral teacher and a good man.

It is impossible for Jesus to have *just* been a good man. He regularly made radical statements such as this one:

Whoever believes in me, believes not in me but in him who sent me. And whoever sees me sees him who sent me. I have come into the world as light, so that whoever believes in me may not remain in darkness. If anyone hears my words and does not keep them, I do not judge him; for I did not come to judge the world but to save the world. The one who rejects me and does not receive my words has a judge; the word that I have spoken will judge him on the last day. For I have not spoken on my own authority, but the Father who sent me has himself given me a commandment—

what to say and what to speak. And I know that his commandment is eternal life. What I say, therefore, I say as the Father has
told me. (John 12:44–50, ESV)

Jesus claimed that believing in Him is the equivalent of believing in
God and that seeing Him is the same as seeing God. He said that He is
the light of the world and that He came to save the world. He pointed out
that anyone who doesn't believe in Him will be judged, that His words
are God's words, and that they are everlasting.

If Jesus wasn't God and wasn't the savior of the world and wasn't all
He claimed, then the label *good man* wouldn't be fitting. Something
more like *liar, freak,* or *fraud* would be far more accurate.

## Be Strong and Courageous

After working through the five questions, you might be asking, *How do
I instill these truths into the heart of my teen and live out the "above all"
command God gave to Joshua?*

We find the answer in Joshua 1: "Be strong and very courageous. Be
careful to obey all the law my servant Moses gave you; do not turn from
it to the right or to the left, that you may be successful wherever you go.
Keep this Book of the Law always on your lips; meditate on it day and
night, so that you may be careful to do everything written in it" (verses
7–8). God told Joshua to follow His laws carefully. This command to
"meditate on" and "be careful to do everything written in" is one requir-
ing a focused discipline.

God wants you and your family to have a well-grounded confidence
in who He is. He knows that this confidence will not take shape without
hard work. My older brother, Kent, just finished running his first mara-
thon. He is fifty years old and understood that getting from the starting

line to the finish line would require strong discipline. He knew that without hard work, he would never be successful. God knew that in order for Joshua to be successful in leading the nation of Israel, he, too, would have to work hard. He would have to *above all* study, know, and reflect on Scripture.

The more you read and meditate on the Bible, the more you believe in God. His Word teaches us how to place confidence in who He is and who He has created us to be. Romans 1:19–20 says, "What may be known about God is plain to them, because God has made it plain to them. For since the creation of the world God's invisible qualities—his eternal power and divine nature—have been clearly seen, being understood from what has been made, so that people are without excuse." And in Psalm 19:1 we read, "The heavens declare the glory of God, and the skies announce what his hands have made" (NCV).

These passages teach us that we can see God's glory, thus placing confidence in who He is, by looking at His creation. Just as our physical eyes see proof of the wonders of the earth, our spiritual eyes see proof of the wonders of who God is. Your teen counts on you to lead him into the wonders of God's Word. Next we will look at how to do exactly that.

# Focusing on What Matters Most

If your family follows sports, you probably can remember who won the last Super Bowl, NBA Championship, and World Series. If you and your teen are gamers, it's quite possible you've had a late night or two hundred challenging your teen with the help of Peach, Daisy, or Lemmy through Choco Island or Mushroom City.

Or maybe your family enjoys music. If so, there is a good chance that whatever the occasion in your house, it almost always includes your favorite playlist in the background. Our family loves all three. Sports, *Mario Kart,* and music all seem to be part of our weekly schedules. We also love meaningless trivia. If your family does as well, you may enjoy questions such as these:

- Which ocean—the Pacific or the Atlantic—is saltier?[1]
- What is America's favorite flavor of ice cream?[2]
- True or false? Babies are born without kneecaps.[3]
- More than thirty thousand Americans injure themselves each year using what?[4]

You may have a few really good trivia questions of your own.

Whether the subject is sports, video games, music, trivia, or something else, have you considered how much knowledge you and your family members possess? I am confident we all know a lot about things that are important to us. I'm also confident we know a lot about things that really don't have any bearing on eternity. In this chapter we'll look at what matters most in life.

In the introduction to this book, I detailed five foundational truths. Let's think of this chapter as "Foundational Truth #6: It's up to you to help your teen know what matters most in life." Your child's first seventeen or eighteen years are the training ground for what's next. You can't control what happens after that, but you can control what you do to prepare your child for life. God has a super-big plan for what is next.

## Your Teen Matters

If I were ranking the struggles of this generation, I would put suffering from low self-confidence and self-worth at the top. I hear questions similar to these almost weekly as I meet teens who lack self-esteem:

- Who am I?
- Do I really matter?
- Am I a mistake?
- Am I important to anyone?

Your teen needs to know that she is no accident and that she possesses great personal significance and meaning. When God made your child, He really was showing off. Look at what Colossians 1:16 says: "Through his power all things were made—things in heaven and on earth, things seen and unseen, all powers, authorities, lords, and rulers. All things were made through Christ and for Christ" (NCV). The key words here, of course, are *all things*. That means everything about your teen matters to God. Her goals, aspirations, weaknesses, challenges, desires, ambitions, choices, relationships—all things in the past, present, and future—matter to Him.

Stacey, a high school senior, approached me at a Youth for Christ event. "I'm really freaked about next year," she said. "I know that God has a plan for me, but I'm nervous about figuring it all out." I encouraged her to work at enjoying her senior year. The questions she has and the uncertainties she feels about what follows high school are normal. God wants to teach her to trust Him during all this because she matters to Him.

Middle school and high school can be scary. Let your teenager know he doesn't face the uncertain future alone. No matter how he might have failed in the past, no matter the regrets, the past does not dictate his future with God. Psalm 139:16 says, "Your eyes saw my unformed body; all the days ordained for me were written in your book before one of them came to be." God will do what He desires to do with your teen. Your child has a God-given purpose, and God wants to help fulfill that purpose because he matters to Him.

## Time with God Matters

Countless teens have shared with me some of their most intimate thoughts and struggles. Each year I receive many letters on just about any topic you can imagine. Here's what Grayson had to say:

> Dear Jeffrey,
>     I'm fifteen and in tenth grade. I am a Christian and have a great relationship with my parents, but I can't say that I feel close to God. I've tried praying and reading my Bible, but I don't stick to it. Help!
>     Thanks,
>     Grayson

My response to any teen who shares a similar story is "Stay the course. Stay in the Word. Stay in communication with God, and it will get better!" Time with God matters. Grab a snack to share with your teen this week and be ready to talk this over. When you do, here are some great questions to ask:

- How much focused time have you spent with God in the past few weeks?
- Are you satisfied with the amount of focused time that you give Him?
- If not, what things in your life are inhibiting you from giving God more of your time?
- What steps might you consider taking to commit yourself to focusing more of your time on Him each day?

To answer these questions, it's also important to consider how one quantifies time spent with God. For me, spending focused time with God is something I try to do every day. I don't always do it, but it is my daily goal to get alone, get quiet, silence my phone, and focus my attention on God. I try to mix up how I spend my time with Him: reading my Bible, meditating on Scripture, journaling, and praying are ways I work to focus my full energy on Him. Of course, as Christ followers, our entire lives should be about focusing all we are on Him. However, making a concerted effort to get alone and get focused on God is really the goal.

If your teen is having a tough time answering these four questions, consider helping her talk through a strategy for spending time alone with God. Does she need a devotional book? You might suggest she use a devotional app. Our ministry has one called Grow On, which is customizable and sends users daily scripture based on a ten-question spiritual assessment. Best of all, it's free in the Apple App Store and on Google Play.

The more time your teen spends with God, the more he gets to know Him, His love, and His will for his life. It will be impossible for teens to know and do God's will if they are not spending time with Him. Here's a great family conversation to have tonight during dinner. Ask your teen these questions:

- Where do you see yourself in five to ten years?
- Where will you be working?
- What kind of car will you drive?
- In what city will you live?
- Who will you marry?
- What house will you buy?
- What investments will you make?
- In what church will you serve?
- How will you use your finances to support a family, give to church and charities, and save for retirement?

These questions are just a few of the many big ones teens will be asking in the next few years. Then ask, "Do you have all the answers to these questions?"

The answer, of course, is no. There would be no adventure, no surprises, and, for sure, no need for God if she knew it all ahead of time. Your teen wants to know the answers to the biggest questions about the rest of her life. We all do. Though no one can deliver the answers, the Bible assures us that spending time with God matters.

Look at Psalm 119:104–105: "Through your precepts I get understanding; therefore I hate every false way. Your word is a lamp to my feet and a light to my path" (ESV). Psalm 119 makes it clear that by spending time in the Word, we will gain knowledge and understanding about what matters most. Because we don't know the future, time with God matters. The more time your teen spends with Him, the more he will learn to trust God about his future, regardless of what answers God chooses to provide.

If your teen hasn't made time with God a priority, encourage her not to give up. The important thing is to commit now to making this happen. If she doesn't begin giving God time each day, she will never know Him as He desires to be known.

God clothes the grass in the field, which is alive today but tomorrow is thrown into the fire. So you can be even more sure that God will clothe you. Don't have so little faith! Don't worry and say, 'What will we eat?' or 'What will we drink?' or 'What will we wear?' The people who don't know God keep trying to get these things, and your Father in heaven knows you need them. Seek first God's kingdom and what God wants. Then all your other needs will be met as well. (Matthew 6:30–33, NCV)

In short, seek Him first. Giving God first priority in life begins with giving Him your time. I received this Facebook message from a high school junior: "I've been getting into the Word more like you challenged us to at camp. You were so right! The more I'm in it, the more I get it. The more I get it, the more able I am to live it!"

## Trusting God with Your All

You probably are familiar with the story Jesus told in Matthew 25:14–30 about the man who gave money to his servants before leaving on a journey. This story is often called the parable of the talents: "To one he gave five talents, to another two, to another one, to each according to his ability" (verse 15, ESV). This passage highlights several things you can teach your teen about what it means to give his all to God.

### God Wants to Give Your Teen What He Will Never Deserve

When we were boys, my older brother, Kent, and I were spending the week at my grandparents' house. I had a fight with my brother, something to do with a chocolate chip cookie. My grandfather, whom we called Pepa, stepped in and sent Kent and me to different rooms to cool down and think about how we had acted. Then Pepa invited us onto the back porch with him for a postfight cookie and some milk.

Obviously, neither of us deserved that cookie, but Pepa offered it because he loved us. Though he may never have fully known it, Pepa had blessed Kent and me. Likewise, the man in Matthew 25 didn't have to give his servants anything. He did so because he wanted to bless them. The same is true with God. He doesn't owe your teen anything, but He does want him to be blessed.

There is a misconception known as entitlement permeating teen culture. Many teens believe they deserve *anything* they want, the *way* they want it, *when* they want it. The truth is that the only thing each of us deserves is hell. We don't deserve anything good. But God loves us so much that He wants us to get what we don't deserve. Talk to your teen about God's desire to bless him with His very best even though he doesn't deserve anything from Him.

## God Wants to Use Your Teen in Unique Ways

The man in Jesus's story (who represents God) gives each servant an amount of money, sometimes referred to as "talents," according to each servant's ability. Because all people aren't the same, the man didn't give the same amount to each one.

God has blessed your teen with certain abilities and talents. In doing so, He has made your child unlike anyone else. God has something for your teen to do that no one else can do better. Given that we as individuals are all unique, we can't compare with others what we look like, where we live, how much money we earn, or what we accomplish in life. Unique means unique.

There always are those who compare people with others. Work hard to help free your teen from the comparison trap. Comparing herself to other people will only fuel her perceived inadequacy. God made your teen to be unique, and He makes no mistakes.

## God Wants to Teach Your Teen to Work Wisely

The man in the parable of the talents left town expecting his servants to work wisely by investing the money he had given them. I don't expect my daughters to do everything perfectly. I do expect them to work wisely each day in everything they do.

Amy and I are intentional about delegating weekly chores to our girls. By doing so, we teach them that work is part of life. It's important for your kid and mine to learn the responsibility of working wisely. We all know that schoolwork puts tremendous demands on kids. I believe that giving my girls responsibilities at home teaches them how to better apply themselves in the classroom. Such responsibilities teach them how to multitask and develop time-management skills.

## God Wants Your Teen to Do Her Part

The man in Matthew 25 had expectations for all three of his servants. He returned from his journey and wasn't thrilled with the news from the third servant. The third servant had done nothing with what had been given to him. Fear, laziness, and apathy probably played a part in his choice not to work hard for his master. The result was that the one who did nothing got nothing.

We read these words in 2 Thessalonians 3:10–13:

Even when we were with you, we gave you this rule: "The one who is unwilling to work shall not eat."

We hear that some among you are idle and disruptive. They are not busy; they are busybodies. Such people we command and urge in the Lord Jesus Christ to settle down and earn the food they eat. And as for you, brothers and sisters, never tire of doing what is good.

God expects us to work hard in all we do. As we work, we are to use the gifts He has given us for His glory. Colossians 3:17 says, "Whatever you do, whether in word or deed, do it all in the name of the Lord Jesus, giving thanks to God the Father through him." In school, at work, with friends and colleagues, when everyone is watching or when no one is watching, God always expects the same thing from your teen: "Give it all you've got!"

### God Doesn't Require Your Teen to Have All the Answers

The master never told his servants when, or even if, he would return. They had no idea what the future held or whether their jobs would continue. I can imagine they questioned if their master was even still alive. They likely wondered where they would find work if something happened to him. Scripture tells us he was away for a long time. I imagine it wasn't easy on the servants waking up every day to the unknown. But it wasn't up to them to know the entirety of the story. Their only responsibility was to care for what had been entrusted to them.

There will be moments in your teen's life when it seems there are no immediate answers to his questions about school, friends, finances, marriage, and a career. This is where trust in God will be critical.

Throughout Scripture we read stories in which God's people had to learn to trust Him. I wish that when I was a teen someone had told me this important truth: you can't trust the situation or your feelings in the moment, but you always can trust that God has your best interests at heart.

## God Wants to Reward Your Teen's Work Ethic

The master rewarded the efforts of the first and second servants. He celebrated their accomplishments by giving them even more. Ecclesiastes 2:24 says, "A person can do nothing better than to eat and drink and find satisfaction in their own toil. This too, I see, is from the hand of God." When you give God your all, He honors you and gives you satisfaction. Help your teen learn what it means to plan, strategize, work, and commit to God all that she does. Proverbs 16:3 says, "Commit to the LORD whatever you do, and he will establish your plans."

## Your Teen's Calling from Jesus Matters

Here's another family-meal conversation idea: encourage each family member to verbalize all the ways God has blessed him or her. Have each one think for a moment about all the great things that have happened in his or her life. Here are a few examples:

- I'm alive.
- I have a family that loves me.
- I have some really cool stuff that makes life fun: my iPhone, my laptop, Netflix, and *Mario Kart*!
- I am saved from hell because I have given my life to Jesus.

God created your teen. He has greatness in store for your child, and He wants to give him abundant life (see John 10:10). What a privilege it is to know God and to be certain He loves us. What a privilege it is to share God's love with people who don't know Him as savior. This is what your teen is called to do.

God might lead your child into ministry or to an occupation that is not defined by the world's standards as an occupation. But as a Christ follower, your teen's number one job is to share Jesus with the world. This was the heartbeat of Jesus. Take a look at the first commission Jesus gave to those who would follow Him: "When Jesus was walking by Lake Galilee, he saw Simon and his brother Andrew throwing a net into the lake because they were fishermen. Jesus said to them, 'Come follow me, and I will make you fish for people'" (Mark 1:16–17, NCV).

Now take a look at the last commission Jesus gave to all Christ followers: "Jesus came and spoke to them, saying, 'All authority has been given to Me in heaven and on earth. Go therefore and make disciples of all the nations, baptizing them in the name of the Father and of the Son and of the Holy Spirit, teaching them to observe all things that I have commanded you; and lo, I am with you always, even to the end of the age'" (Matthew 28:18–20, NKJV).

Do you see the resemblance between these two commands? I can summarize the passages in the word *go*! Evangelism was extremely important to Jesus, and it must be important to every Christian.

Your teen probably knows someone who is not a Christian. I do. I have two neighbors who are not Christians. I see them frequently. They know that my wife, children, and I are Christians. I believe that God has placed us in our neighborhood, in part, so we can point our neighbors to Christ. We've had really interesting conversations about God. They haven't yet given their lives to Him, but I am hopeful they will surrender to Jesus one day. Satan wants your kid to feel fear when it comes to sharing Jesus with people. But God wants her to experience a sense of how fabulous it is to share the gospel.

There's no greater privilege than sharing the saving message of Jesus with someone else. In chapter 17 I'll share some steps you can follow to help encourage and empower your teen to share his faith. Talking to a person about Jesus may seem impossible, but when God calls teens to do something, He gives them everything they need for the task.

We read in 1 Corinthians 1:25, "The foolishness of God is wiser than men, and the weakness of God is stronger than men" (NKJV). Even in God's so-called weakness, He's still stronger than the greatest human strength. Remind your teen that she is not alone. When God asks something of a person, He provides the way, the words, the courage, and the outcome. Make sure your teen knows that her life speaks much more loudly than mere words. Your teen gives witness to Jesus even without opening her mouth.

Ask God to give your teen His eyes, His ears, and His heart to see the world as He sees it: desperate for hope, love, and God. Pray that he will see interactions with people as opportunities to share Jesus. Pray that he will start to grasp the urgency to be a voice of truth and light in a world seemingly running from both. Pray that his aspiration won't simply be to gain knowledge but rather to answer the call of Jesus to "go."

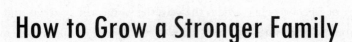

# How to Grow a Stronger Family

My wife is an amazing attorney and a wonderful teacher. She has taught law for many years at our alma mater in Nashville as an adjunct professor. Several years after she began teaching, Amy told me she loved being in the classroom more than in the courtroom. She said it made her feel alive to stand in a lecture hall in front of college students, helping them grow intellectually, professionally, and spiritually.

Thirteen years later she was offered a tenure-track position as a university professor. At times, the journey of waiting was a trying one for our family, but we never stopped trusting, praying, reading Scripture, and following God's direction. Amy knows this is her mission field. She knows she has a platform to not only inspire students in the classroom with head knowledge but also combine that knowledge with spiritual truth that will prepare students to be everything God wants them to be.

We know that God formed our family—Jeffrey, Amy, Bailey, and Brynnan—to strive to *above all* lean into God and trust that He has our best interests at heart. You can cultivate growth and strength in your family, but it is essential that you do the following:

1. Spend time together doing things that bring you closer to one another.

2. Read and meditate on Scripture, both as a family and as individuals.

3. See prayer as a vital daily practice that orients your hearts toward God.

4. Spend time with others who prioritize the Word and prayer.

## It Begins with Priorities

Two things I hope to never forget from my childhood are that my family almost always had dinner together and that my dad often would read the Bible and my mom would pray before we left the table. My family spent quality time together, we spent time in the Word together, and we spent time praying together.

If spending time together is not a priority for your family, all of you will suffer. Satan wants nothing more than for you to neglect spiritual disciplines such as Bible reading and prayer. Your family counts on you to communicate these truths and lead by example, so commit to living by these principles. Here are a few more ideas for growing a strong family.

### Model for Your Teen That the Word Is the Way

We read in 2 Timothy 3:16–17, "All Scripture is God-breathed and is useful for teaching, rebuking, correcting and training in righteousness, so that the servant of God may be thoroughly equipped for every good work." There is no worldly success that can replace what God's Word can do for your child. If you are not reading the Bible as a family, there is a strong possibility some members of your family are not in the Word. Many teens see the Bible as archaic, irrelevant, or hard to understand. I believe this is a direct result of the fact that they spend little, if any, time reading God's Word.

Over the past several years as I have traveled to speak to a variety of groups, I have been heartbroken to see fewer and fewer people holding a Bible. Although some now have their Bibles on their mobile devices, I have seen a tremendous decline in the number of people who bring any kind of Bible to Christian events. Increasingly, I see a lack of knowledge of God's Word and a lack of desire on the part of Christians to grow in their knowledge of it.

How would each of your family members answer these two questions?

1. Is the Bible important to our family?
2. How do we as a family incorporate the Bible into our lives?

Why not ask the members of your family these questions tonight? Let their answers dictate what you do next.

### Establish a Family Devotional Time

I spoke recently at a parenting conference, where I met Rick, a husband and father to three preteen boys. He told me about the fun his sons have with devotional night. He said, "Some weeks I will read from the devotional book we are using, and other weeks one of my sons or my wife will read. We read from the New International Version, *The Message,* or the New King James Version. I work to keep it different so that it keeps my boys engaged."

It's important that you make this time a consistent part of your schedule and that every member of the family understands that participation is nonnegotiable. It's easy to say you don't have time to read the Bible together. If you haven't been able to stick to a plan, that's okay. What is important is that you are trying. But know that the more you work to make it happen, the more Satan will throw obstacles in your path. You have to get to the place where family devotional time is a priority for everyone. This may mean that some weeks you gather on Tuesday nights, while the next week it's on Thursday morning before school. You will need to be creative so that your devotional time is engaging and is a regular part of your family's life.

### Get Every Family Member a Bible

You won't become a strong family until each family member has his or her own Bible. I recommend choosing a modern version. If you have a preteen, consider getting an age-appropriate Bible she will enjoy reading. If your teen has spent little to no time reading the Bible, get a translation that is simple and easy to understand. Take her to a bookstore to look at different Bible versions and read sample passages. I enjoy reading *The Message,* which is a paraphrase of the Bible written in a relatable way. I also recommend the New International Version and the Holman Christian Standard Bible.

Do what it takes to help your teen connect with God's Word. A new Bible will not guarantee that your child will consistently read the Word or apply it to his life. But by instituting a comprehensive plan to prioritize Scripture and apply it to real life, you will send a strong message about what's important.

### Help Your Teen Begin Her Personal Faith Journey

Your teen needs to understand that the journey toward God won't happen automatically. She has to take the steps to grow in walking with Him. Encourage your teen to seek out resources—whether books, apps, videos, or websites—that will equip her for ongoing spiritual growth. I wrote a book for teen boys called *Watch This* and one for teen girls called *This Is Me,* both of which tackle pressing teen issues from a biblical perspective. At the end of each chapter, I included questions that work well as conversation starters. There are many other great teen devotional books available as well.

Perhaps your whole family will select a book, read it together, and then discuss it. Each week family members could read one chapter on their own and then convene as a family to discuss the impact the chapter had on each family member. Video-driven devotionals and small-group studies are other options for launching good discussions.

Of course, there will be days when your teen chooses not to spend time with God. Be careful not to push too hard or criticize, as this may prompt her to ignore Scripture altogether. But do try to encourage consistency and help her find a method that works.

### Encourage a Bible-Reading Plan

Take a look at Psalm 119:104–105: "I gain understanding from your precepts. . . . Your word is a lamp for my feet, a light on my path." When you read Scripture, you gain understanding. As the members of your family commit to spending time in the Word, they'll develop a greater understanding of who God is and He will more clearly reveal His plan and purpose for each of their lives.

If you google Bible-reading plans, you will get pages of results. Both biblegateway.com and bible.com have plans that could give your teen a kick start to get into the Bible each day.

For years I've told teens about the 1:1:1 plan, which involves reading one passage once a day for one week. The cool thing about this plan is that you get to decide on the passage, which can be one verse or many verses. This plan is all about repetition (you end up reading the same passage seven times). Often I read the Bible and immediately forget what I've read. Or my mind wanders while I'm reading and I start thinking about all the things I have to get done. Reading the same passage each day for a week helps me absorb the truth of Scripture.

Psalm 119:9–11 explains the importance of absorbing what you read:

How can a young person stay on the path of purity?
By living according to your word.
I seek you with all my heart;
do not let me stray from your commands.
I have hidden your word in my heart
that I might not sin against you.

A person can live in the right way by "living according to [God's] word" (verse 9). The passage then gives the million-dollar solution to sin, the top struggle in our lives: "I have hidden your word in my heart that I might not sin against you" (verse 11).

How can you help your teen avoid sin? By ensuring that he is memorizing Scripture! The 1:1:1 plan will help with this. When I use this plan, I often find that I don't even have to open my Bible at the end of a week because I already have the passage memorized.

You can use this plan as a family by choosing a passage for the coming week and then encouraging each family member to use the plan. How cool it would be if your whole family could recite the passage by the end of the week!

## Help Your Teen Develop a Love for the Bible

Spending time with God works to our benefit. As your teen spends time reading the Word, she will gain understanding from God about life, love, relationships, and purpose. The more we are in the Word, the more the Word gets into us. Amy displays scripture throughout our home, often on a card or as a handwritten note. The Word of God is visible to anyone who walks through our house, especially our daughters.

Proverbs 30:5 says, "Every word of God is true. He guards those who come to him for safety" (NCV). God promises that when you read and meditate on His Word, He will provide safety and protection. Don't we want our kids to learn to take refuge in God? If you haven't already done so, pick a few Bible verses and display them throughout your home. (You can write them on sticky notes or index cards or use another method that works best for you.) Equip your child with God's truths by displaying His Word throughout your home.

### Keep a Family Prayer Journal

Mark 11:24 says, "I tell you, whatever you ask in prayer, believe that you have received it, and it will be yours" (ESV). Moses, Abraham, Joshua, David, Paul, and even Jesus spent time praying. Teaching your teen to pray will be one of the most powerful lessons you can instill. Remember, you and your spouse are the most influential people in his life, and he learns how to live by watching you.

A family prayer journal can be a powerful tool for documenting God's faithfulness to your family. We keep our journal in the living room. It is packed with memories of our prayers and family celebrations. The great thing about journaling is that you get to decide the format. If journaling is new to your family, here are a few suggestions:

- **Journal the specifics.** When you write down your prayer requests, be specific. You may want to assign a separate color of ink to each family member. This way you can look back on the prayer requests to see who wrote what and when.
- **Journal with gratitude.** Teaching our kids to pray for more than their wants and needs can be a powerful lesson in prayer. Remember to journal about things for which you are thankful just as much as you journal about the things you hope God will do for you.
- **Journal your questions.** At times my girls ask me questions I can't immediately answer. Amy and I make a point of

teaching our girls to take their questions to God. We also model this in part by journaling our prayers for wisdom and guidance.

- **Journal big dreams.** As you dream big for your family, encourage family members to do the same. Writing down your hopes for such things as healing, a new job, or clarity on a big decision can help you focus on the things you want to accomplish, as well as the areas of your life that need to be tweaked.

- **Journal answered prayers.** Keeping a record of God's faithfulness will provide memorable affirmations of His goodness to your family.

## Find Targeted Scriptures for Specific Struggles

A teen whose parents are divorced sent me this message: "I've started implementing what you told us about at Winter Xtreme to find specific scriptures for specific struggles. I found Psalm 4:4: 'Don't sin by letting anger control you. Think about it overnight and remain silent' [NLT]. My struggle with anger isn't resolved, but I do feel better. I've put this verse on the inside of my locker at school so I read it every morning. I wish things were different at home. They aren't. But Scripture is helping me deal with my anger. Thank you!"

I often suggest that teens find Bible verses that address their specific struggles. Encourage your teen to find verses that help with challenges she is facing. The internet can be a tremendous resource for finding applicable verses and passages. You and your teen can find scriptural help by searching "scriptures for dealing with anger" or "verses on depression." What a great rhythm to get into while she is young, teaching that God's Word is real and relevant for every area of life.

### Spend Time in Prayer

As your teen commits time to reading the Bible, prayer likely will become a greater part of his life as well. As 1 Thessalonians 5:17 says, "Pray continually." Explain that we all can and should pray at any time.

It also is important to help your teen realize there are many different ways to pray. Prayer is not about having a once-a-day ritual, nor is it merely a habit of thanking God before a meal. Prayer is a lifestyle of communication with God, talking to Him anywhere and about anything. A father of three came up with this great idea:

> During our family devotional times, we recently started encouraging our teens to email their prayers to God. We came up with a bogus address, and each teen would take five minutes at the end of their devotional time to send an email to God. I think they began to put a lot more thought into their words, and it made prayer more real and intimate for them, like they were communicating with a friend. The neat thing is that five minutes eventually became six, and then eight, and then ten.

God wants us to be honest, sincere, and real with Him. Prayer offers your teen the opportunity to do that.

### Spend Time in Creative Prayer

Several years ago our family experienced challenges unlike any we had faced before. I knew my daughters would remember this season, and I wanted to make sure what they remembered most wasn't the struggle but rather the decision our family made to trust God.

Prayer had to be a focal point. Amy and I started praying in creative ways. We would sit on one of our daughters' beds at night to pray as a family. We still do that. I started praying with my girls in the morning as

I drove them to school. I prayed for their day, their safety, and their influence on others. We still do this.

One night the four of us went outdoors and walked around our house and prayed. We took four laps around the house, each of us taking a turn to pray. We still take regular prayer walks, sometimes around our house or around our neighborhood or even around the building where my wife works.

I encourage you to walk, talk, and pray regularly with your family. Look for creative ways to pray. The message will become clear: talking with God is something you can do in any way and at any time.

### Spend Time Listening

Proverbs 1:5 says, "Let the wise listen and add to their learning, and let the discerning get guidance." Getting to know God requires not only talking to Him but also listening to Him. Often Satan puts in overtime to get us to buy lies such as *You can't hear God. It's ridiculous to even imagine that He would talk to you.*

One teen told me, "Last week at camp you talked about hearing the voice of God. Jeffrey, I've been a Christian for almost ten years, and I don't think I've ever heard God's voice." My response was "Neither have I—not audibly, anyway. But I know He communicates with me." The question is not whether God speaks but whether we choose to listen. We have to teach our children how to train their ears to listen to God speaking through the Holy Spirit.

What does God's voice sound like? He can speak to us through something as subtle as a pang of conscience. Your teen has probably faced a temptation to drink alcohol, gossip, smoke pot, or cheat on a test. She probably stopped to consider the choice. Even if only for a moment, your teen felt something that reminded her of the right thing to do. That was the Holy Spirit speaking. His words may not be audible, but His truths are always loud and clear. Teach your teen that this is one very clear way in which God speaks.

An integral part of learning to hear God is trusting Him with every area of life. Each of us can be guilty of wanting God only when we need Him or when our world is falling apart. Teens in particular can be guilty of looking to God only when friends have hurt them, when a big test is looming, or when a huge pimple appears on the morning of prom. Yet they often fail to trust Him during the good days. Your role is to help your child see you as one who trusts God with all your heart so she will do the same.

## Spend Time with People Who Love God

We know several families whose kids are close in age to Bailey and Brynnan. We invite them into our home regularly to share a meal or simply to fellowship together. We laugh a lot, talk about God, and pray. In doing this we have learned the importance of spending time with others who love and serve God. Whether we realize it or not, we need one another.

Acts 2:46 reads, "The believers met together in the Temple every day. They ate together in their homes, happy to share their food with joyful hearts" (NCV). Spending time with other believers has shown our daughters that other families, like ours, know the importance of spending time with God, reading the Word, and praying. It also has provided them with opportunities to share about their personal walks with the Lord. Reading the Bible and praying with other people aren't always easy, but the more we are with families that do the same, the more our girls get comfortable talking about their faith.

## Spend Time with People You Don't Know

For years we have hosted an open house during the month of December. We invite our neighbors, and every year we meet people we've never met before. My family gets to know people who live near us. This simple act has shown our girls what it means to reach out to people and share the love of Jesus. It has also ignited conversations with our daughters about the importance of community, outreach, evangelism, and prayer for friends, neighbors, community, and the world.

## Just Get Started

If you have not spent much time in the Word, in prayer, or with other Christians, I encourage you to begin now. It may not feel as though you have any time to spare, but these simple steps might be the boost you need:

1. Commit fifteen minutes a week to reading the Bible and praying together as a family. Don't worry so much about developing a devotional plan from the outset. Just set aside fifteen minutes this week to begin to build this discipline consistently into your family's schedule, one week at a time.

2. Let your teen pick out a notebook to use as the family prayer journal. Place the notebook in a high-traffic area, such as your family room, kitchen, or dining room. Seeing the notebook will encourage your family members to grab it, write in it, and pray.

3. Establish parameters that you all agree to follow during family devotional time. These might include no television and no mobile devices. Also, plan to have a different family member lead your family time each week. Doing so will keep your conversation fresh while teaching everyone the importance of leading a group discussion and being creative with the content and direction of the conversation.

4. Pray. Begin praying now that God will protect your family from distractions as you commit to spending regular time together. Satan will work hard to disrupt this time, but you will prevail if you remain determined and prayerful.

I know that I need all the parenting help I can get from God. I also know that my ability to parent is only as strong as my willingness to surrender time to Him. Matthew 6:30–33 states,

> If that is how God clothes the grass of the field, which is here today and tomorrow is thrown into the fire, will he not much more clothe you—you of little faith? So do not worry, saying, 'What shall we eat?' or 'What shall we drink?' or 'What shall we wear?' For the pagans run after all these things, and your heavenly Father knows that you need them. But seek first his kingdom and his righteousness, and all these things will be given to you as well.

As you work to apply the principles from this chapter, find confidence in knowing that God also is doing His best for you and is helping you establish a strong family.

# The Critical Role of a Father

H ello, my name is Inigo Montoya. You killed my father. Prepare to die." If you are smiling, it's possible you are remembering this classic scene from the 1987 film *The Princess Bride.*[1] At the top of the list of my favorite scenes from this movie is the one when Inigo finally avenges his father's death. Inigo has waited his entire life to find his father's killer, recite these important words, and exact his revenge. During the fight scene the count begs for mercy and offers Inigo money, power, anything he wants in exchange for sparing his life. But what Inigo most wanted was his father.

If you have a strong relationship with your father, you know the confidence, strength, and security this relationship has given you. Even if your relationship with your father isn't what you'd like it to be, it has shaped you in profound ways, and you probably still long for a good relationship with him. I regularly meet teens who are either looking to a father for love and support or seeking something or someone to fill the void left by an absent father. In this chapter I want to talk directly to dads. I'll speak to moms in the next one.

Dad, I believe four words capture the heart's desire of nearly every teen: "I want my father." He is desperate for the participation of an involved father. Consider this question as it relates to your parenting: "Can I do more?" At this moment, as I contemplate this question about my own parenting, I am answering, "Yes!" I know I can do more. I need to be more involved, more engaged, more intentional, and more focused. Although I do well in some areas, I need work in others. As you read this chapter, keep asking yourself, *Can I do more?*

## Finding Ways to Do More

My kids—and yours—can have the opportunity to model their lives after a father who is brave, loving, and determined to do the right thing in every situation. As our kids observe us, they learn how to live. Remember God's challenge to Joshua, that *above all* he was to "be strong and very courageous . . . careful to obey all the law my servant Moses gave you" (Joshua 1:7). Twenty-three chapters later in the book of Joshua, we see that Joshua finally got it.

Standing in front of more than one million people who were following his lead, Joshua told the nation of Israel, "If serving the LORD seems undesirable to you, then choose for yourselves this day whom you will serve, whether the gods your ancestors served beyond the Euphrates, or the gods of the Amorites, in whose land you are living. But as for me and my household, we will serve the LORD" (24:15).

The nation of Israel, and more importantly Joshua's family, heard his proclamation. How would your wife and children feel if they heard you make this bold commitment? Our families count on us to serve the Lord completely. Your teen will learn what it means to serve the Lord as she observes and follows your lead. So how do you live in a way that is worth following? Let me suggest nine ways.

### 1. Prioritize Time with God
Habakkuk 2:1 reads, "I will stand like a guard to watch and place myself at the tower. I will wait to see what [God] will say to me" (NCV). In

chapter 5 we discussed practical ways to help your family engage with God's Word. The truth is that your ability to lead your family begins with your willingness to let God lead you. Unless you make spending time alone with Him a priority, you never will be the spiritual leader your family needs. I have found that the more time I spend alone with God, the more I'm able to facilitate spiritually robust moments for my family.

If you are anything like me, your days feel too full and your responsibilities too great. But you and I are chosen by God to lead our respective families, which means this is one responsibility we can't afford to ignore. In Matthew 14:23 we read that Jesus "went up on a mountainside by himself to pray." We know this was a habit for Jesus. The Bible mentions numerous instances when Jesus prayed. If the Savior of the world needed time with His heavenly Father, how much more do we?

As you spend time with God in prayer and in His Word, He will better prepare you to be an effective leader in your home. Don't worry too much about the place you use for spending time with God. Concentrate instead on being diligent in meeting with Him regularly. I retreat to my home office in the morning since the house is usually quiet at that time. Schedule consistent time each day to listen to God, refocus your priorities, reenergize your commitment as a father, reaffirm your life purpose, and retune your heart to God's voice.

## 2. Handle Conflict Wisely

Proverbs 10:19 teaches, "If you talk a lot, you are sure to sin; if you are wise, you will keep quiet" (NCV). King Solomon was reminding us that our words matter. Several years ago I got into a heated conversation with Amy on Christmas Day. I don't remember what our disagreement was, but Bailey and Brynnan have never forgotten it. Numerous times since, both girls have reminded me of *that* Christmas. Of course, no family can completely avoid disagreements and heated moments.

When a conflict arises, your role is to seek to defuse the situation and look for a peaceful resolution. Often I find it helpful to be the first to admit fault and apologize. Even if you feel that it wasn't your fault, it's more than likely that you shared some of the blame. Do everything you can to handle heated moments wisely, seeking to follow the advice of Proverbs 21:23: "Whoever keeps his mouth and his tongue keeps himself out of trouble" (ESV). Our kids learn how to deal with conflict by watching how *we* deal with heated moments.

A father told me that he and his son were having trouble getting on the same page regarding some choices his son was making. "Every time we talk about it," the father said, "it feels like World War III." I encouraged him to

- set healthy boundaries for discussion that he and his son could work toward, such as no screaming and no storming out of the room
- hit pause on the conversation when either of them was angry until they both have calmed down
- work to find common ground
- respect each other even when they don't agree[2]

## 3. Speak Love

King Solomon wrote often about the power of our words. Here is one bit of wisdom: "Gracious words are a honeycomb, sweet to the soul and healing to the bones" (Proverbs 16:24). Also, "A word fitly spoken is like apples of gold in a setting of silver" (25:11, ESV). I have seen the impact of speaking love to my girls. It visibly changes how they view themselves.

One of the most powerful attributes you possess as a father is your influence over your child. When you say uplifting and encouraging words, you help develop confidence and self-worth. At some point every day, I try to tell my girls these things:

- "You are beautiful."
- "You can do anything you set your mind to."
- "I am so proud of you."
- "I love you."

Job 4:4 reminds us that our words can be especially uplifting when our child is struggling: "Your words have comforted those who fell, and you have strengthened those who could not stand" (NCV). Work hard to speak love to your teen and help shape his beliefs, convictions, and self-worth in profound ways.

## 4. Establish the Right Atmosphere

Satan wants my family and yours to stay busy, because a busy family often is a disconnected family. As a dad, you have the job of establishing the atmosphere in your home. And when I say *atmosphere,* I mean an environment in your home that protects your family time while honoring God. Atmosphere can include determining how often your teen uses mobile and handheld devices, the amount of time your family spends doing "family things," and the priority you place on praying as a family. Atmosphere also includes family time devoted to talking about global and cultural events, the church, and the world; and the frequency and timing of family meals. Of course, atmosphere also encompasses when you vacation, which nonprofits your family supports, and even what parties and gatherings you host as you reach out to the world around you.

Every home is different, and what works in one may not in another. Here are a few questions to consider as you think about your role in establishing the atmosphere in your home:

- How will you protect your family from movie, music, and media influences that do not align with Scripture?
- What limits will you place on activities such as playing video games, watching television, and spending time on social media?

- Does your family have a mission statement that details the kind of family you want to be and the kind of outreach you want to embrace as a family?

I work hard to create a family-focused atmosphere. I have instituted regular family game nights, movie nights, and devotional nights. The older our daughters get, the more creative I have to be to protect our family time. Both Bailey and Brynnan play soccer and basketball. That means our family schedule is completely different during the fall than it is in the winter. In the fall, soccer games are on Tuesday and Thursday nights. In the winter months, the girls play basketball on Monday and Friday nights. Sunday nights have become our family's regular Netflix-and-popcorn night. We all know to clear our schedules because Sunday is a nonnegotiable night reserved for just the four of us.

Our family nights, game nights, and shared mealtimes ebb and flow as our daughters' schedules shift throughout the school year. We adjust as needed to accommodate their busy lives while protecting our time together.

## 5. Attend Church Together

It is good for your teen to attend church. It is even better for her to know that church is a priority in your life and for you to go to church together.

One parent wrote to me, "My daughter thinks church is boring. She's given it a try, but she doesn't like the youth group and says the other teens ignore her. Should I let her stay home, or should I make her go?" My answer: it depends.

It's common for teens to find church boring and for youth groups to be cliquish and unwelcoming. Some teens use this as an excuse to sleep in on Sundays, and you need to recognize when this is the case. For other teens, though, there are legitimate concerns.

You may need to assess the authenticity and effectiveness of your church's youth program. Don't force church on your teen; instead, take action in positive ways. Talk with adult volunteers in the youth department. Take your youth pastor out for coffee. If the leaders are unresponsive to your concerns, you are unsatisfied with what you discover, or your teen continues to express valid concerns about church and the youth group, you may need to search out other alternatives.

Only after much consideration, prayer, and confirmation from God should a family change churches. The key is to find a Bible-believing church where you can grow and serve as a family. It might be necessary to send your teen to another church for youth group if it is in her best interest and will encourage a deeper relationship with God.

## 6. Take Charge in Communication

Show your teen you believe in him. Making time for consistent communication with your child does wonders. Because teenagers typically don't go to parents asking to talk about important subjects, you may have to work creatively to bring up the serious stuff. If you do not talk with him about the hard issues, who will?

Talking about sex, pornography, school life, and peer pressure may not be the easiest and most comfortable conversations you'll ever have. But what's important is not how comfortable you are; it's that your teen trusts your involvement in his life. When you proactively communicate authentic biblical truths, you teach him how to discern between truth and lies.

Sixteen-year-old Stephen said, "I have been struggling with lust since I was in eighth grade. It's embarrassing and I don't know what to do. My dad is so involved at church—he probably would die if I talked to him about all this. But I wish I could."

Stephen's dad probably isn't intentionally avoiding the issue; he's just not making the effort to invite open communication. This dad doesn't realize that by not being approachable and letting his son know he can handle difficult topics, his son has to try to figure out his struggle on his own. If your teen can't come to you with hard issues, he will go somewhere else for help.

Spend time every day talking with your teen, even about general or inconsequential things. You can talk while playing ball, working in the yard, driving somewhere, or watching TV. Maybe he won't talk at first. But the more you talk, the more he will view you as trustworthy. The more he trusts you, the more he will open up to you.

## 7. Invest in One-on-One Time

Get away from work and other demands and hang out one on one with your teen. Pick a night once a week, every other week, or whenever you feel like it, and have fun together. See a movie. Play basketball. Ride go-carts. Go hiking, swimming, shopping, skiing, hunting. Get a pizza or play miniature golf. Do something she enjoys.

My older daughter loves movies. My younger daughter likes to get her nails done. I'll admit, I've discovered that a foot massage is pretty awesome. These moments together create memories that will last a lifetime. When I ask teens for one way they would improve their relationships with their dads, they most often respond, "Spend more time together!" Have you ever said things such as these to yourself?

- *I know I promised my son I'd be at his game, but this work meeting could make or break my career.*
- *I don't really need to spend time in the Word with my kids. I'm tired tonight. Plus, isn't that why our church hired a youth pastor?*
- *I'd better not ask my daughter too many questions about who she's going out with and where they're going. She may think I'm being nosy. If she wants to talk, she'll come to me.*

- *I'd better not bring up that subject with my son. He'll
  figure it out on his own. I figured things out, didn't I?*

I've missed many moments when I wanted to be there for my girls. There are times when work calls and we have to answer. But you and I have only eighteen years with each of our kids, and then they're out of the house and on their own. This is why prioritizing time with them is critical. Time leads to communication, and communication leads to having a positive impact on your teen's life.

### 8. Teach Your Son to Respect Women

What are you teaching your son in regard to how he should treat women? Your son will treat women the way *you* treat women. He also watches the examples set by our culture. Movies, television, and other forms of entertainment frequently depict disrespect toward women as acceptable, even humorous. We see people working out their differences using insults and put-downs. Boys are taught to be jerks to one another and to women. In such an environment I can think of no greater example of godly manhood for your teen than Jesus.

John 19:25–27 reads, "Near the cross of Jesus stood his mother. . . . When Jesus saw his mother there, and the disciple whom he loved standing nearby, he said to her, 'Woman, here is your son,' and to the disciple, 'Here is your mother.' From that time on, this disciple took her into his home." Jesus had been beaten, spit on, stripped of His clothes, cursed, slapped, kicked, mocked, ridiculed, and then nailed to a cross. Yet just moments before He breathed His last, He was more concerned about His mother than about His pain. What an incredible act and example for all men.

Jesus made respect cool. You can help your son see that respect is still cool, particularly when it comes to honoring women.

In recent months a number of stories have surfaced about men—

often in powerful positions—who took advantage of women. In only a few of these cases have we heard the accused admit, "I was wrong and I am sorry." You must have a conversation with your son about how to behave toward women. Obviously, you hope he never will treat a woman disrespectfully in any way, especially sexually. However, if he does, choosing to be less than forthcoming (which is, in fact, lying) about his actions is equally disrespectful and abusive.

We have to teach our sons what it means to respect women. We also must teach our sons never to run from their poor choices but instead to do the honorable thing, take responsibility for their actions, apologize, and do whatever else is needed to help the victim begin to heal.

It is critical that you help your son understand that it is never okay to disrespect any woman. Ever. Not only should he follow Jesus's actions by respecting all women with whom he comes in contact, but he should also protect them. On a date, he should never place any girl in a situation where there is the potential for harm. This includes never parking alone in an isolated place, being careful about the movies they watch, never taking advantage of her sexually, never requesting nude pictures from her, and avoiding parties where there are drugs and alcohol. This also includes choosing to never disrespect a woman by looking at porn. No, he doesn't know the woman on the screen, but he doesn't have to know her to disrespect her. Have you communicated these things to your son?

## 9. Teach Security and Significance to Your Daughter

When my daughter Bailey was five, she gave me a birthday card she had made herself. The card read, "Dear Daddy, Bailey loves you very much. I will always be your best friend forever. Even when I am older, I will always love you and be your best friend. Love, Bailey." I still remind her of that card all the time. I should probably have the card laminated so I can wear it around my neck when her friends come over.

When she wrote this card, Bailey hadn't even started kindergarten. Now that she is a teenager, she relies on me more than ever before to help her feel secure. Before, she wanted affirmation when she drew a picture. Now she wants affirmation about her grades, her friendships, and so on. She wants me to celebrate her successes. She smiles when I tell her how beautiful she is. She loves it when I pray with her. If she is having a bad day, she wants me right there beside her to comfort her. She has given me the honor of occupying a special place in her heart.

You will always be your daughter's hero, no matter her age. She may not run and jump into your arms, but she still needs you to make her feel special, secure, and significant. She still needs you to say with your life, your time, and your involvement, "I believe in you."

In this world, teen girls receive many confusing and often misleading messages, and many feel pressure to fit in by wearing the right makeup and hairstyle, conforming to the dictates of fashion, having the right body type, and dating the right guy. Here are a few of the lies Satan tries to use to distract or destroy your daughter:

- To be popular with the boys, you need to dress sexy.
- Guys only love skinny girls. Go ahead and purge.
- You absolutely must have a boyfriend to feel secure.
- Never talk to your parents about anything. They won't understand.

What's a dad to do? First, realize your daughter needs you. Even if she never tells you so, she needs you to remain involved in her life. Satan wants you to believe that your daughter is her mom's responsibility. But it's your biblical responsibility to provide support and affirmation. Second, develop a game plan for involvement in her life. You know your daughter's likes and dislikes. You know her favorite foods, music, movies, and stores. (If you don't, ask her mom.) Now take the knowledge you have and set aside time to do something with your daughter that she enjoys.

A father told me, "One night a month is for just me and Kiley. We go out, we eat, and we see a movie or go watch a game. We grab coffee and we make a date of it. I'll admit it was a little awkward for us both at first, but we've been doing this for two years now, and we've never been closer. She talks to me and shares things I never dreamed she would. She has this place in her life that she lets me into. She leaves for college this year, and I will cherish forever these past two years spending time together."

What if your first outing doesn't go smoothly? Take it slow and build trust one step at a time. Demonstrate that you're interested in her. Ask your daughter what she would like to do. Tell her that you just want to be together. Maybe you institute a monthly father-daughter date night where you go out for ice cream. Sometimes it's as simple as asking how her day went, giving her a hug, or telling her she's beautiful. Or perhaps you write her a letter telling her what she means to you.

As a father, you play a critical role in making your daughter feel loved, needed, and secure. Live in such a way that she has no doubt that you believe in her. Of course, her ultimate security and significance will come from her relationship with God. But you are the father God chose for your daughter, and you have a powerful and irreplaceable role in her life.

## A Quick Word About Sports

Growing up, I played football, baseball, and basketball. There were plenty of fumbles, missed catches, dropped pop-ups, strikeouts, and air balls. From the first time my dad saw me hold a baseball bat, he probably realized I would never make it as a pro. Even so, I knew that my dad was proud of me. How did I know? He told me.

Your teen longs to know that you are proud of him regardless of his ability. He wants a real connection with you that is never dependent on talent or skill.

I met Zach when I was speaking on the West Coast. He is a high school football player who had committed to playing NCAA D-1 football in California. Zach said, "I kind of feel like I missed out on normal conversations with my dad growing up. We seldom talked about anything other than sports. I sometimes wish I could have had a normal life growing up doing stuff with my dad other than sports."

If your teen is an athlete, it is important for you to reinforce constantly that your love is not based on her performance on the field or court. Teens with athletic ability are often praised for their achievements. But what happens when their achievements do not measure up? There is nothing wrong with encouraging and challenging your teen to be the best at any task she faces, but you must also communicate that no matter what happens in the game, you are well pleased with her.

What about teens who have no interest in sports? Teens, especially boys, are often assessed by their athletic ability. However, many teens have amazing abilities in other areas. Your teen needs to know it is okay if playing sports isn't his thing. Have you told him this?

## Freedom from Fear

Remember when your child was young and had nightmares? She would shuffle into your bedroom in the middle of the night, asking you to slay the bogeyman. You were the monster hunter, and nothing could hurt her when you were around. You may need to provide that same sort of reassurance today. I find that even if it's not the bogeyman, most teens fear something or someone.

Rebecca, age fifteen, told me, "I live with fear every day. I want to talk to my dad about it, but I'm not sure he will get it. I wish that for just one day he could feel my fears. Then he would understand what I live with."

I have counseled many teens who live with constant fear. Maybe it's the fear of not having the newest, coolest stuff. Maybe it's the fear of rejection, betrayal, or loneliness. Some fear they will lose their solid family structure through the death of a loved one or their parents' divorce. Others fear failing, being different, being laughed at, or not mattering. These kinds of fears are real.

Teens also have fears that you might not expect. One teen said, "I love it when Mom lets us have a party at our house. Then I know certain things aren't going to happen that I might be tempted to do while at my friends' homes."

Another told me, "My spiritual life could really sink when I graduate and move away. Without my parents to get me out of bed on Sunday mornings, I'll probably have a hard time getting up for church."

These teens were expressing fear that they would not make good choices once they were out of their parents' home. Do you know what your teen fears most? Have you ever talked to him about his fears? Start talking. Your child may be waiting for you to initiate a conversation that could be the first step toward freedom from fear.

## The Call of a Father

Satan is working overtime to convince you that your teen doesn't need you as much as when she was younger. He also wants you to believe that everything else in your life is more important than your teen—your status within your community, your friendships, and your job. The fact is, nothing is more important than the impact you have on her life.

God chose you to be a father to your child, but maybe life feels out of control. Maybe you're more distant from him than ever before. Maybe you feel you can never become the father he needs. Maybe you think it's too late to win back your teen. Maybe you think he is in a good place and you can coast through the next few years. If you believe these lies, the Enemy has you where he wants you: ready to turn and run, ready to coast, or ready to surrender.

Your teen needs you! Don't listen to the lies. Seize the moment and keep praying, striving, and working to be the father God chose you to be.

# 7

# The Critical Role of a Mother

I recall one spring from my boyhood when we'd had so much rain that the street in front of our house flooded. My brother and I ran through the streets barefoot, playing tag in water up to our knees. All we wore that day was our underwear.

In first grade I broke a finger. The following year I broke an arm. There was a broken big toe in fourth grade, a bruised elbow in fifth grade, and a damaging skateboard wreck in sixth grade. I remember having my appendix removed when I was a senior in high school. When I was a kid, I spent a good amount of time at the emergency room.

When I was a freshman in high school, I performed a Barry Manilow song in the talent show at our school. I've been trying to forget that experience ever since.

The same thread runs through every injury, every accomplishment, every ball game, every celebration and tragedy, and every breakup: my mom was always there to comfort me, to listen to me, to encourage me, and to provide a trustworthy presence.

Mom built godly strength into my life. Today my mother and I don't live in the same city and I don't see her every day, but not a day goes by that I don't benefit from the influence she provided. I am the person of character I am today, in part, because of my mom.

You, too, can be a mom who positively shapes character in your teen's life. In this chapter we'll look at specific ways you can support your teen. God has a special calling for you.

## Just for Moms

It doesn't matter if you're a stay-at-home mother or if you work outside the home—chances are good that you take responsibility for much of the hands-on interaction with your child. You're in the kitchen more when she wants to talk. You keep a more watchful eye on her daily interactions. You probably do most of the driving to and from soccer and dance practice. You probably buy her toothpaste and deodorant and know what size shoes she wears. It isn't that fathers never know what's going on; it's just that mothers seem to have a special bond with their children, an intuition that keeps them in touch in ways dads often aren't.

Because of their increased day-to-day interaction, mothers often get the harder parts of raising teens. You're around your child more, so he becomes more familiar with you. Maybe you find that you get brushed off more or teased more or talked back to more. It seems that many of the teens I've talked with take their moms for granted. When I asked them about this, here's what some of them said:

- "Sure, Mom does a lot for me. I probably don't appreciate her as much as I should." (Elaina, seventeen)
- "It seems like I can get away with more stuff with my mom. Dad's always serious. It's like if he puts his foot down, we know he really means it. But with Mom, we can kind of push her to the limit." (Jasmine, fourteen)

- "Mom had this chart she made for us to keep track of our chores and stuff. But it didn't last very long because my brother and I started making fun of it. So after a while she said 'whatever' and that was the end of the chart." (Wyatt, thirteen)

When your kid is a teen, you may not always receive the appreciation you deserve, but there's a good chance your hard work will pay off in years to come. She may not articulate how much she appreciates you until after becoming an adult. Or she may never say anything, but you (and her dad) will have the satisfaction of knowing that you rose to the incredibly hard yet rewarding challenge of being a mother.

## A Godly Approach to Motherhood

Consider the godly mothering demonstrated by Hannah, the mother of Samuel, one of Israel's greatest prophets. Even before Samuel was born, Hannah was praying for him. I hope you will take time to read her story (see 1 Samuel 1:1–2:11, 18–21).

Initially, Hannah wasn't able to bear children, which was disgraceful in that culture. For years she prayed for a baby. Finally, God answered her prayer, and Hannah conceived and gave birth to a son. Her hope was fulfilled at last. But here's where the story takes a twist. After she weaned her child, Hannah made good on a promise she had made to God before Samuel was born. Hannah took her young son to the temple, where she dedicated him to God. Then she left him there. From that moment on, Eli the priest raised Samuel at the temple. (To be clear, I'm not suggesting you take your child to church, dedicate him to God, and then leave. Though I'm sure there are days . . .)

This story demonstrates a number of distinctive characteristics of Hannah's parenting style. She lived thousands of years ago, but God's truth is always relevant. By looking at Hannah's life, we can learn important truths about what it means to help our kids every step of the way.

## A Mother Never Stops Praying

For years things hadn't been going Hannah's way. Her husband's other wife, Peninnah, ridiculed Hannah because she was barren. Satan worked hard to convince Hannah that God would not grant her the desires of her heart. But she never stopped praying. She never gave up on God. She believed that God could answer prayer, and she resolved to give her situation to Him.

It might seem that your timing and God's aren't in sync. Maybe you are in distress over what appears to be unanswered prayers concerning your life or the life of your teen. Hannah's story is a reminder that God's timing is never wrong.

God's plan was fulfilled exactly as He desired in Hannah's life. Even though Hannah couldn't see the big picture, she still believed that God was in control. Scripture tells us that Hannah was in "great anguish and grief" (1 Samuel 1:16). But even in her anguish she continually went to God in prayer.

Time spent with God in prayer is critical for winning the battles we face personally and those our children face. Psalm 34:17 declares, "The righteous cry out, and the LORD hears them; he delivers them from all their troubles." Along the same lines, in 1 John 5:14–15, we read, "This is the confidence that we have toward him, that if we ask anything according to his will he hears us. And if we know that he hears us in whatever we ask, we know that we have the requests that we have asked of him" (ESV).

No matter what circumstances you face with your teen, the example of Hannah shows you can know that God has everything under control.

## A Mother Maintains Her Integrity

Year after year, Hannah endured the jeers of her husband's other wife. Finally, she had a son and did what she promised she would do. Rejoicing over the gift of a son, she took Samuel to the temple to live. She gave up the one thing she wanted most in life.

Having integrity means being devoted to doing what's right. If you wonder what has happened to integrity in our day, look at a few emails I've received.

A fourteen-year-old boy wrote, "Jeffrey, I look at porn almost every night on my computer in my room. The funny thing is, I'm basically okay with it. I'm not concerned that what I'm doing is wrong, because what I'm doing works for me. What else am I supposed to do at this age? I believe that God is okay with my lifestyle because it doesn't harm anybody. Isn't that what morals are about—not hurting anybody else?"

An eighth-grade girl wrote, "Yeah, I've cheated [in school] a few times. But what's the big deal? It's just a lousy test, and doesn't everybody do it from time to time?"

A sixteen-year-old boy wrote, "I've taken my Honda up to 125 miles per hour on the street, and I think it will go faster. All my friends and I are into street racing and seeing how fast we can get our cars to go. There's a side of me that knows this is wrong, but laws are meant to be broken. Isn't that what Jesus did?"

In these emails, teenagers attempt to redefine integrity. They are essentially saying, *Look, as long as I can justify what I'm doing, then what I'm doing is okay.* Their words reveal the pervasive influence of relativism. Adhering to high moral principles regardless of circumstances is a choice that many teens are either unaware of or defiant about. But this is an area where you can influence your teenager.

Your teen needs to see you consistently exhibit integrity so she will understand that integrity is essential to honoring God. As Proverbs 10:9

says, "Whoever walks in integrity walks securely, but whoever takes crooked paths will be found out."

## A Mother Controls the Calendar

After leaving Samuel in Eli's care, Hannah no longer saw her son regularly. But she was still active in his life. We read in 1 Samuel 2:19 that "each year his mother made him a little robe and took it to him when she went up with her husband to offer the annual sacrifice." Hannah, eventually the mother of six children, had a packed schedule. With the responsibility of taking care of five kids at home, it would have been easy for her to forfeit her responsibility to Samuel. But she didn't. That took tremendous discipline on her part.

The Enemy works to create distance between parents and teens through perpetual busyness. He convinces families that it's okay to fill the calendar as long as they're filling it with good things. A packed calendar is the top excuse most parents use to explain why they don't spend more time with their children.

As a mom, you must control your family's calendar. There is a huge difference between actively connecting with your teen and staying busy with the trappings of teen life. You have to draw the line when you begin to sacrifice relational intimacy in order to fulfill the demands of your schedule. I'm all for allowing kids to enjoy activities that are important to them, but there will come a point (sooner than you can imagine) when your teen will no longer live in your home. You have a narrow window of opportunity to influence his life in the areas that matter most. This is why you can't compromise in controlling the family calendar.

If you need to regain a sane schedule, establish a plan with your husband and then have a family meeting. Don't be surprised if your teen responds unfavorably. If you have given her free rein in the past to participate in every single activity or opportunity, expect opposition when you announce your new plan to control the calendar. But stay the course. *No* is not always the easiest word to use, but it is often the best word.

Be prepared for temptation to arise. As you commit to controlling the calendar, Satan will try to take you down Guilt Trip Highway. He will try to convince you that it's okay to say yes to another commitment "just this once." If you choose not to, he will do everything he can to make you feel guilty for saying no. Don't let him win. Saying no to another activity on your calendar is actually saying yes to time with your teen.

### A Mother Expresses Her Love

I like to imagine that every time Hannah took Samuel a new robe, she hid a note in each pocket. I think this way because my mom did that repeatedly while I was growing up. I can't recall everything she wrote in her notes, but I smile even now as I think about sitting on my bed reading them. Often I would open my lunch box and find an "I love you" note next to my peanut butter and jelly sandwich.

My mom still expresses her love to me in creative ways. Just yesterday I received this text from her: "God is faithful even when I don't understand what He is doing. Trust Him and He will provide for you each day. I am so proud to be your mother and love watching the man you have become." I am forty-nine years old. As far back as I can remember, my mom has been sending love notes. I hope she never stops.

This past weekend Brynnan asked me to help her clean out the drawer of her bedside table. If you knew Brynnan, you would know why I essentially had to clear my calendar for the day. She keeps everything. During the next few hours, I saw an unfathomable number of pencils, stickers, pictures, and sticks of lip balm. Guess what else was in the drawer? Brynnan had saved many of the love notes Amy had written to her. I cried as I read each of these letters and saw the love Amy had spoken into Brynnan's life.

It may not be love notes or handmade robes, but you have an opportunity to express love to your child in beautiful and caring ways. You probably have your own way of communicating love. If you don't, it's not too late to start. A quick text or a note in a lunch box or on a bathroom mirror are just a few of the ways you can creatively remind your teen how much you love him.

## A Mother Understands the Importance of Legacy

Even before my daughters were born, Amy and I prayed that God would use our children to do remarkable things for Him. This is what Hannah prayed for her son in 1 Samuel 1:27–28: "I prayed for this child, and the LORD has granted me what I asked of him. So now I give him to the LORD. For his whole life he will be given over to the LORD."

When Hannah prayed, "I give him to the LORD," she was praying that Samuel would leave a legacy worth remembering for generations to come. Look at what the Bible says about the legacy this man left: "The LORD was with Samuel as he grew up; he did not let any of Samuel's messages fail to come true. Then all Israel, from Dan to Beersheba, knew Samuel was a true prophet of the LORD" (3:19–20, NCV).

Isn't this what we desire most for our children? One of the greatest aspirations Amy and I share is that our daughters find favor with God and leave legacies of significance. Several years after Amy and I were married, we were told we would have trouble having children. We saw several doctors and underwent several procedures, but we continued to remain childless. I clearly remember the February night when, after almost five years of tears and frustration, Amy told me, "I'm pregnant!" I also remember that Amy almost immediately began praying that God would bless us with a child who would bring Him glory. To this day, Amy continues to pray this for both of our daughters. She prays that God will do something special with Bailey and Brynnan that will honor His name and make Him known in the world. I hadn't made the connection until I wrote this chapter that Amy is praying just as Hannah did. My girls' mother asks God to use our children for His work all their lives.

Amy understands how closely prayer and legacy are connected. Do you? Amy tells our girls often that the choices they make will shape the rest of their lives. She's praying they make choices that leave legacies worth following.

### A Mother Chooses Surrender

By bringing her son to the temple, Hannah demonstrated complete faith in God, trusting that Samuel was in God's hands. Hannah's desire to honor God superseded her desire to hold on to her son. Her choice shows that one of our greatest joys comes from being willing to give our children back to God. Even before Samuel took his first breath, Hannah was at peace with the one thing that all mothers must be willing to do: let go.

Hannah continued to involve herself in Samuel's life, doing her part to provide for him as a mother. She also modeled the essential act of surrender. By returning her son to God, Hannah was proclaiming her trust in God's goodness. She believed that God could do more in her son's life than she could do on her own. And Hannah trusted that whatever God chose to do with Samuel's life, God had it all figured out. It could be that God is inviting you to a place of surrender, a place where you are willing to trust Him even though it doesn't make sense. God is good, and it makes sense to *Him*.

## You Will Always Be Mom

My mom called today to tell me she is praying for me. She and I talk often, and there are few, if any, times when we talk that she doesn't ask, "How can I pray for you?"

One of the things I will always remember and cherish is that my mom lifts me up in prayer. Additionally, my mom can talk me through life's challenges in a unique way. I am almost fifty years old, yet when I'm talking with my mom, it's as if I'm ten again. Mom talks to me as if I'm the only person in the world.

As a mom, you occupy a special place in your teen's heart. Use this to your advantage when talking with her. Consider sharing with your teen that you understand what she is going through. Share stories about how you struggled at that age. Share your desire to help her see past the lies of Satan and never compromise, no matter how great the desire to do so. Show her the foundations of God's promises to people who obey Him, as found in Deuteronomy 28:11–13:

> The LORD will grant you abundant prosperity—in the fruit of your womb, the young of your livestock and the crops of your ground—in the land he swore to your ancestors to give you.
>
> The LORD will open the heavens, the storehouse of his bounty, to send rain on your land in season and to bless all the work of your hands. You will lend to many nations but will borrow from none. The LORD will make you the head, not the tail. If you pay attention to the commands of the LORD your God that I give you this day and carefully follow them, you will always be at the top, never at the bottom.

God is inviting you to shape your teen's character in powerful ways. Your role can be a difficult one, but it also is a privileged one. You are called to be on the front lines with your teen, guiding him every step of the way. God has given you a calling that only you can fulfill.

# 8

# How to Keep the Lines of Communication Open

**C**ommunication isn't always easy or fun, especially with a teen. One mom said, "I'm tired of even trying to talk to my teen. Every time I try to talk to her, she acts as though she wants nothing to do with me."

If you can relate, you are not alone. Your teen may not fully understand how much he is wired by God to rely on you. But it's true that our children, even during their teenage years, are designed to depend on us. Have you ever considered this issue from your teen's perspective? Here's what a few teens told me about their struggles to communicate with their parents:

- "It means so much to me when my dad talks to me. I know he's a busy guy, but I actually like hearing what he has to say. Sometimes he's really funny too." (Cameron, eighteen)

- "Just once I wish my mom would ask my opinion about something. She always gives me advice, but she never asks what I think about anything. I've got good things to say too." (Brooke, sixteen)

- "Nobody talks to anybody in my house. The TV is always on. My mom says not to interrupt her during her shows. My dad has to watch the news every night. Then he watches it again on another channel. Then he checks his phone. Then he goes to bed." (Blake, fifteen)

- "Once I tried telling my mother about this joke I pulled on my friend Jake. But I don't think she got it. She just stood there with her mouth open and then told me I needed to apologize to Jake. That's the last time I tell her anything." (Micah, sixteen)

- "My mom is not afraid to say hard things to me. I like that about her, even though I don't show it sometimes." (Lucy, fourteen)

When I ask teens what they would most like to improve about their relationships with their parents, the overwhelming response is time and communication. Effective communication with your teen is a precious skill and a necessary tool in helping her navigate the years of adolescence. As a parent chosen to love and guide your teen, you can do this.

## Avoiding Communication Traps

The first time my wife and I took Bailey to our favorite vacation spot, she hated it. The sand bothered her feet, and the water was big, loud, and scary. On our second trip to the beach with Bailey, she finally got up the courage to stand at the water's edge . . . in her shoes. After a few days of wearing shoes while standing in the water, she wanted her shoes off. By week's end, she was running like crazy on the beach and having a blast.

Over the next few years, she became more and more confident in and around the water. It's easy to see the progression of Bailey's beach experiences. From the time she wouldn't let go of my hand to the times she fought me *to* let go of my hand, we've come a long way from her saying

"The sand hurts my toes" to "Daddy, I'm going to swim out to the sand-bar alone!"

Aren't our relationships with our kids similar to this? As they transition from children to young adults, our kids, in their God-given pursuit of independence, learn to wade more and more deeply into life's waters. Right now your teen may believe he no longer needs you. It may seem he doesn't even want you around (except for food or money).

But you know otherwise. Your teen definitely still needs you. The challenge is to find out what method of communication will be most effective. Countless obstacles and scenarios can leave you and your teen frustrated, angry, and resentful. Think about it. Have you ever had any of the following thoughts?

- *My teen just won't listen to me. I don't know what's going on in her life.*
- *I don't want to be a nag. I'd better just lay off and keep quiet for a while.*
- *I've tried to talk to him before about the music he listens to, but I can't get through to him.*
- *If I talk to her about how she dresses, she'll think I'm old fashioned and uncool.*

We think thoughts similar to these and wonder why it's so hard to find solutions. Talking—and listening—to teens can be hard work. But God has chosen you for this role, so it's possible to break through the barriers. Later we'll look at specific communication techniques, but first let's look at two vital practices that help establish strong communication.

## 1. Strategize

Preparation is an integral step toward improved communication. Take time before you talk to organize your thoughts and develop a plan of action.

As we have discussed, your teen wants an involved parent. He may not always show it, but it's true. If you struggle to communicate well with him, it's time for you to spend more time preparing. Thinking things out in advance will help you take full advantage when an opportunity for communication arises.

Know what you want to say—and why you want to say it—before you say it. Ask yourself questions such as these:

- If conversations in the past have ended poorly, what might I modify about my approach?
- Is there a specific topic I've been avoiding that I need to address with my teen?
- Has God put something on my heart to discuss with my teen but I have not done it? If so, how will I accomplish this? When? Where?
- If I want to say something to my teen, what is my interest in doing so? What's the goal?

## 2. Surrender

God has called you to be a parent who is ready and willing to communicate His truths to your teen. At the same time, Satan fights to convince you that you are neither worthy nor capable of this calling.

I had lunch with a close friend recently who said, "My daughter and I hardly communicate anymore. We used to be so close. Since she started middle school, it feels like she has pulled away more and more. After a while, I kind of felt like I should give up. I guess it's true that once they get older, they no longer need us like they once did."

On some level, most parents can probably identify with this dad. As our kids exercise their independence, it can feel as if they no longer need us. But don't let Satan, the culture, or your teen convince you of this. Your son or daughter needs you as much now as ever.

Psalm 37:7 is a great reminder to "wait and trust the Lord" (NCV). I realize that applying such a verse is easier said than done. If you are having a difficult time communicating with your teen, take your communication concerns to God. I suggest this prayer of surrender:

> *Dear God,*
>
> *I know that my situation with my teen is no surprise to You. I also know that You have created me to be the parent of _____. Right now I surrender our situation to You. I can't do it without Your strength, so I'm asking You to lead me as I strive to parent in a way that brings You glory.*

Your situation is no surprise to God. He wants you to know that no matter how difficult or discouraging it is for you, He plans to use you to speak truth into the life of your teen.

Perhaps the lines of communication between you and your teen are open and you're doing fine. But don't forget that Satan wants nothing more than to disrupt your relationship with her. If this is the case for you, I suggest this prayer of surrender:

> *Dear God,*
>
> *Thank You for giving _____ to me. I need Your guidance every step of the way. I want to surrender our relationship to You. I know that Satan wants to destroy our relationship, so I pray for Your protection. Teach me to be a parent who honors You as I lead my child.*

Wherever you are in your relationship with your teen, you must continue to surrender the relationship to God, asking Him to lead you.

## Healthy Communication Strategies

Shaping a successful plan of action can help in more ways than you might think, especially when dealing with difficult and sensitive issues. These twelve strategies can help you develop a workable plan for healthy communication.

### 1. Shoot Straight

Never shy away from telling the truth. Never. If you and your teen find it difficult to communicate, open up about some of your own struggles. Tell him you know your relationship is changing and you want to be respectful of that. At the same time, convey that you are standing at the water's edge, allowing him to venture farther toward the deep end. Remind him that though you aren't perfect, you are the parent God chose for him. Make it known that you want to do the right thing always.

### 2. Give Advance Notice

If you and your teen need to have a serious conversation, tell her ahead of time. That way you both can prepare for the big talk. Plan a meeting time and place. Have some fun in advance. Send a text or photo suggesting a time and place to meet. If you're Snapchat savvy, consider taking a selfie of your dog and adding a caption such as "Scruffy mentioned that you and I should go for a burger and bring one back for him."

### 3. Take It on the Run If Needed

Sometimes even an important conversation has to take place on the fly. Take advantage of opportunities even if they are brief, such as at breakfast, during the ride home after school, right after you and your teen arrive home, or just before bedtime.

### 4. Know Your Window of Opportunity

You probably have noticed times when your teen is more open to talking. If he is not a morning person, look for a time slot at night. However, if he is pretty much wiped out by nine o'clock each night, find time at breakfast or set up a lunch appointment. Find moments in each day when he is most apt to talk. Get these times on your mental calendar and live by them. They could be the most valuable minutes of your day—and your teen's.

### 5. Engage in Small Talk, Which Can Lead to All Talk

Ten minutes of daily small talk can go far when building a broader level of trust. (You might want to skip ahead to chapter 9 for additional helpful suggestions.) What interests your teen? Sports, music, friends, hobbies? Start there. As she sees that you are interested in the little things, she might begin to confide in you *all* the things that are important.

### 6. Walk and Talk

Some of the best conversations Amy and I have with our daughters take place during evening walks in our neighborhood. When you have something important to discuss, success often depends on a relaxed setting. One mom told me her son loves music, so she found that turning on something he enjoys is a great way to get him talking about his day, his dating life, and more.

When is your teen most relaxed? While on a walk, watching a ball game, playing video games, or spending a day on the boat with you? Helping create an environment that is comfortable, relaxing, and fun for him will promote openness and a sense of security.

### 7. Be Prepared for Anything

Teenagers have shared with me things I'd never have imagined would come out of their mouths. When you make yourself available and your teen begins to see you as a person worthy of her trust, you might be surprised at how much she shares. Get ready!

## 8. Show Your Curiosity

If your teen isn't naturally a talkative, self-disclosing kid, you might begin by asking questions. Ask open-ended questions that can't be answered with *yes, no,* or *maybe.* If he comes home angry or upset over something that happened at school, instead of asking, "Do you want to talk about it?" focus instead on questions that lead to a broader response. Try "What happened today that made you feel this way?"

## 9. Put Down the Device

The leading complaint I hear from teens as it relates to parents' lack of attention has to do with cell phones. Teens say something like "My mom is always on Facebook. That's all she does!" Or "My dad never puts his phone down. I wish he gave me as much attention as he does Candy Crush." Think about the amount of time you are on your phone. What message are you sending to your family, particularly your teen? I try hard to put away my phone when I pick my girls up from school. I want them to know that when they get in the car, nothing is more important to me than talking to them and seeing how their days went.

## 10. Hit Pause When Necessary

Kids can ask questions that leave us perplexed. If uncomfortable topics come up with your teen, it's okay to pause and consider your response. Take the matter to God; discuss the topic with a spouse, friend, or pastor; and then revisit it with your teen.

Being a connected parent doesn't mean you always have all the right answers and advice. Tell your child you need time to consider the topic. Settle on a time when the two of you will continue the conversation.

Then stick to your word and approach the subject again after you have considered it thoroughly.

## 11. Write Notes

Communication is more than just oral. Written communication can allow you the opportunity to express your convictions more clearly and with less inhibition. If you have not had a long, deep conversation with your teen recently, a personal note from you might be exactly what is needed. A heartfelt note can pave the way for great face-to-face conversations down the line.

## 12. Avoid Avoidance

If you choose not to talk to your teen about a particularly difficult topic, you should realize you are sending a message. Topics such as sex, masturbation, homosexuality, and divorce sometimes are treated as taboo subjects. If you ignore these or other topics, assuming your teen will figure it out on her own, trouble could be right around the corner.

Several years ago I counseled Michael, a teenage boy contemplating suicide. His desire to end his life was the product of an ongoing struggle with porn that had begun years earlier. He shared that his father, a pastor, would not discuss the matter. His dad's silence left him feeling alone, confused, dirty, and worthless.

## Keep the Communication Lines Open

Many teens are hungry for help and guidance. Again, discussing such matters may be uncomfortable for you. But failing to do so could be much more harmful because culture often fills in where you fail. No matter how inadequate, underprepared, uncomfortable, or uninvolved you may feel, remember that you are the most influential person in your teen's life. If you choose not to communicate, he will search elsewhere for answers.

It may appear to you that the last thing your teen wants is a conversation. You may have tried for years to connect. You might feel that you have already implemented many of the ideas in this chapter, only to hear silence.

Keep trying. Continue to develop your strategy and surrender it to God. No matter how difficult the moment is, it is your moment. God has made you for this moment, and He is with you every step of the way. Keep talking!

# 9

# Getting the Most out of Dinnertime

Dinnertime can be one of your best opportunities to talk as a family. Yet for most families, the evening meal has become the forgotten time. Many families aren't home for dinner at the same time, or they eat on the run as each family member scatters to various activities.

My wife and I have to fight to keep dinnertime a consistent family time. Our daughters each play three sports and are involved in student government, choir, and youth group. And, of course, they have homework. There are nights when we can't all be home for dinner. Through the years we've gotten creative at protecting this time.

If dinnertime seems to have become the forgotten time for your family, you might need to undertake a dinnertime makeover. Take a close look at your family's calendar. Develop a weekly dinnertime schedule that takes into account meetings, study groups, rehearsals, games, work, and so forth. Some nights, dinner has to happen at a restaurant or maybe on the fly between events. Establish a realistic plan to have dinner together as a family on a consistent basis.

Recently, Amy, the girls, and I were eating at a restaurant. At the table next to ours, every person in a group of five was on his or her phone. No one was talking. Instead, they were all eating with one hand while holding their phones with the other.

I often hear parents complain about distracted dining. Remember, you are the parent. You decide what dinnertime looks like for your family. Though there will be times when you have to deviate from it, create a plan and enforce rules that will make dinnertime a consistent family time. Here are five of my family's nonnegotiables:

1. Eat at the table, not in the living room.
2. No television.
3. No cell phones.
4. Pray before you eat.
5. Talk about your day.

Sitting at the table forces us to face one another. The seating arrangement encourages either conversation or extended, awkward silence. Eventually, it will be more interesting to have a conversation. If you can, begin the practice of praying before a meal when your kids are young. Proverbs 22:6 reads, "Start children off on the way they should go, and even when they are old they will not turn from it."

Amy and I look for imaginative ways to get our girls talking. It goes without saying that some children talk more than others. And just because they communicate well with you today doesn't mean they'll want to talk tomorrow. We make it a point to discuss school, work, the world, friends, social media, politics, and religion. We also try to mix it up. Every spring the NCAA releases the brackets for the March Madness basketball tournament. Several years ago we began our own March Madness tradition. The night before the first games of the tournament begin, we print four copies of the brackets, go to a restaurant, and each complete a bracket, choosing the final team we think will win the tournament. Though we often don't know all the teams that enter the tourney, and rarely do all of us pick the winning team, we enjoy discussing basketball and our picks for the tournament.

Talking as a family sends the message to your teen that "Mom and

Dad are invested in what's important to you." Once you get your kids talking, you never know what you'll hear.

## Prompts for More Meaningful Family Conversations

It's sometimes difficult to know how to get good conversations going, especially if you have not made dinnertime conversation a family rhythm. Here are twelve conversation starters you can use to facilitate energetic table talk.

### 1. What happened today?

My daughters love recounting their days, telling us everything that happened. We started asking about their days when they were in elementary school. They are now in high school and still tell us about what happened at school. If your child is a preteen, now is the perfect time to begin asking, "What happened today?" If she is a teen, give it a try anyway. My girls love seeing that Amy and I are interested in hearing about their experiences.

### 2. What is one thing you did today to make someone else's day better?

It's easy for parents to focus on the major issues, such as "Don't have sex," "Say no to drugs," "Don't look at porn," "Come straight home after the movie," and "Where will you be tonight and who else will be there?" Yet we often miss minor matters and details that are equally important, such as teaching our kids kindness and compassion for others, how to have a servant's heart, and good etiquette.

Parents need to major on the minors with our kids, reminding them that every day they have opportunities to make someone's day better. Brynnan recently texted to tell me she gave a doughnut to a girl at school.

The girl had had some struggles at home and had posted alarming comments on social media. I know that being given a doughnut was a kindness the girl appreciated.

### 3. Who did you sit with at lunch?

Just as it's important to know who your kid's social media connections are, it's critical to know about his daily connections in the real world. A mom told me she began asking her daughter about the people who sat at her lunch table when her daughter was in elementary school. Now that her daughter is in middle school, this mom says, "I learn so much about her friends by asking, 'Who did you sit by today?'" If your child reports that he sat alone, follow up, as this may reveal a deeper issue at school that you need to address.

### 4. What's on your mind?

Make it clear that your teen can talk to you about anything and that you'll listen. It's important that our kids feel they can talk openly and share whatever may be on their minds. If communication has not flowed freely in the past, it might be tough for your teen to answer the question "What's on your mind?" Consider answering the question yourself. Talk about what's on your mind—work, family issues, or the latest movie you want the family to see. The topics don't have to be serious or heavy. The more you talk, the more your teen will feel invited to do so as well.

### 5. Can I tell you about something that happened to me today?

Often, getting kids to talk begins with taking the focus off them. Many nights Amy and I initiate the conversation by talking about what happened to us that day. This sends the message to our kids that life is about more than them.

As our kids learn the art of talking, they also need to learn the art of listening. There are times when the moment is right to relay a message to my kids about something I want them to know. For instance, I received an email from a distraught parent who has a son in serious trouble. The boy had encouraged his girlfriend to send him nude pics of her, and his girlfriend sent several. This young man then forwarded the images to several of his friends, and the pics went viral. Once the boy hit Send, by Louisiana law he had distributed child pornography (see chapter 11 for more on responsible cell phone usage).

I was able to remind my daughters of the dangers of sexting. Our conversation that night was an extremely robust one about purity, sex, and pornography. My daughters engaged in this conversation partly because I presented what I wanted them to know in a conversational way rather than as a formal teaching moment.

## 6. What's on our schedule for the next few days?

This may seem unimportant, but based on conversations I've had with teens, I know this question is one of the most important on this list. Your family probably hits the ground running at the start of every day. Many teens tell me they are clueless about the everyday things their parents and siblings do. Likewise, they say their parents rarely check in on their personal lives, homework, or dating.

Taking time to talk through each family member's planned activities is an important part of staying connected. I encourage you to ask this question more often. In doing so, you send the message that you want to know what's up in your teen's world. Amy is good at keeping everyone's agenda front and center. As part of this effort, she asks this question almost every night at dinner. If your child is young, it's important to involve her now in making plans for the family, such as the schedule for tomorrow or the weekend or the plans for the next family vacation. It's equally important to let every family member know that his or her schedule is important to Mom and Dad.

## 7. What's going on in the world that is interesting to you?

One of my college professors challenged students to read an article every day from the local, national, and international sections of the newspaper. I still maintain this practice using online news sources. Helping our kids develop cultural and global awareness is one of the greatest gifts we can give them. Learning about the world is the first step to caring about the world.

This generation will interact with people from most parts of the globe in college and in the workplace just as a matter of course. Being aware of global events and diverse cultures will prepare our kids to be "witnesses to [Christ] in Jerusalem, and in all Judea and Samaria, and to the end of the earth" (Acts 1:8, NKJV). Asking questions such as this one encourages our kids to think beyond their own interests and concerns while teaching them the importance of developing a globally responsible worldview.

## 8. What are you grateful for today?

Psalm 100:4–5 issues an important reminder to be grateful for everything God has done for us: "Enter into His gates with thanksgiving, and into His courts with praise. Be thankful to Him, and bless His name. For the LORD is good; His mercy is everlasting, and His truth endures to all generations" (NKJV).

Do you consider yourself a positive or negative person? I'd always considered myself a positive person, until one day Amy told me I was a negative one. Over the next few days, I was more conscious of my actions and comments. I hadn't noticed it, but once Amy pointed it out, I saw that I had allowed some situations to steal my joy and gratitude.

Now I try hard to be grateful for my life, no matter my circumstances. I want to teach my kids to be grateful and to express their gratitude. This question invites your teen to really think about his life, blessings, health, and friends and then formulate a positive statement that captures gratitude.

Paul wrote in Philippians 4:8 that "whatever is true, whatever is noble, whatever is right, whatever is pure, whatever is lovely, whatever is admirable—if anything is excellent or praiseworthy—think about such things." We do best when we focus on what's positive rather than what's negative. Get into the rhythm of asking your teen to answer this question. As she thinks through reasons for gratitude, her mind will be filled with thankfulness.

## 9. Are you concerned about any of your friends?

We have had countless conversations about our daughters' friends. We've learned a lot about not only their friends but also teen culture. As our girls tell us about their friends' interests, celebrations, and struggles, Amy and I get to know their friends better. We usually just listen and offer support, advice, or encouragement as needed. Sometimes we have to give direction and biblical guidance as our girls consider which friends to spend time with, which parties to stay away from, and so on. There are also times when I try hard not to show that I'm shocked and speechless. The more we engage our girls in conversation about people, issues, and dilemmas, the more they see us as trustworthy. And trust, of course, leads to a greater willingness to talk openly about the people and things important to them.

## 10. What do you want to do with your life?

Read what a teen named Kimberly wrote: "I wish my parents affirmed me more. They really are great parents, and they've helped me so much getting through school, with homework and everything. It feels like we talk a lot about all the things I shouldn't do but rarely about my dreams and goals and desires."

Teens often tell me they would love to have more verbal support from their parents, especially about their futures. I have to remind myself that my girls need affirmation as it relates to their aspirations. Bailey and Brynnan need to know that, second to God, Amy and I are their biggest fans. We want them to succeed at whatever they do. Success for them begins with the confidence we speak into them. Continue asking your teen what he wants to do in the future. As you do that, you will instill in him the confidence to go for it and to become everything he desires to be.

## 11. For which concerns, needs, and struggles can we pray for one another?

This question tells your teen that you love her so much that you want to take her needs, concerns, doubts, and anxieties to God. Every time we have asked our daughters this question, they have had an answer.

Have you ever asked your child, "How can I pray for you?" No matter the age, everyone finds comfort in knowing that someone is praying for him or her. Asking this question can lead to meaningful conversations that can go in any number of directions. One night I asked this question, and it resulted in our praying for people on our daughters' campus who may not be Christians. If you haven't asked this question before, why not try it tonight?

## 12. How can I be a better parent?

In one of my favorite movies, *Field of Dreams,* Kevin Costner's character keeps hearing a voice whisper, "If you build it, he will come."[1] Get ready because if you ask it, she will answer! Asking such a question isn't for the weak of heart. If you do ask how you can become a better parent, you may hear something you don't want to hear.

You also might hear exactly what you need to hear. I had never thought about asking my daughters this question until I was writing this chapter. I'm a little afraid of how they might answer. But I also know that asking them might make them aware that their opinion is important to me. I guess this means I need to tell Amy that I have the next question ready for dinnertime tonight.

If asking questions at the dinner table is new for your family, take it slow. Consider asking one question tonight. If you don't get the response you want, don't force it. Also, don't give up. Try again tomorrow night. I'm confident that in time your family will grow closer and more self-disclosing as you all begin to talk. Happy eating!

# Navigating Our Media-Driven World

A few years ago Bailey came into my office, closed the door, and told me she needed to ask me a serious question. "Is it true that guys think about sex every seventeen seconds?"

You can imagine my shock, as well as the self-discipline it took to contain my laughter. "What?" I asked. She then repeated her question.

I told her I wasn't sure of the answer, even though I was thinking, *It's probably more like every ten seconds.* I asked where she had heard such information.

"The internet," she replied. She had been doing research for a school paper. On the browser home page, an ad popped up displaying the statistic she had quoted. Our conversation reminded me that I *have* to be involved in my teens' digital lives.

Let's keep in mind that the real enemy of the family is not the world. "Our struggle is not against flesh and blood, but against the rulers, against the authorities, against the powers of this dark world and against the spiritual forces of evil in the heavenly realms" (Ephesians 6:12). Jesus reminded His followers, "The thief comes only to steal and kill and destroy" (John 10:10). The liar and thief is Satan, who is working to deceive your teen. He uses powerful tools such as social media, movies, music, television, commercials, magazines, the internet, and video games. The harmful messages teens encounter are filled with lies.

The entertainment industry pushes the boundaries further every year. Television shows glamorize dirty jokes, partial nudity, homosexual messages, anti-Christian sentiment, and disrespect for life, parents, committed relationships, marriage, and God. Articles and ads in teen magazines tell girls that their looks are their only ticket to security. Teen boys are told that if they drink the right beer, own expensive cars, and wear the right body spray, women will fall all over them.

Then there is the world *wild* web. Along with the internet's many benefits comes a pervasive message that anything goes. This generation accepts pretty much anything, especially when it comes to morality and spirituality. Even if some teens don't take part in immoral acts or practice alternative religions themselves, many of them don't see anything wrong with these harmful things. When teens consume a steady entertainment diet that promotes violence, illicit sexual activity, rebellion, hatred, arrogance, and other forms of worldly excess, this spills over into their behavior. It's the old "Garbage in, garbage out" adage from the world of computer programming. And if their behavior is not changed, at the very least they will become desensitized to these things.

## What to Do About Media Madness

What teens read, watch, and listen to is much more than entertainment. The onslaught of media messages affects how they think, act, make choices, and ultimately live their lives. As an adult, you already have formed your worldview. But your teen is forming his belief system right now. Your child needs your guidance because he lacks the maturity and life experience necessary to filter the madness. It's your responsibility to help him recognize deception for what it is.

We can't throw caution to the wind and hope our teens will get it right. We need to do what we can to combat the madness by presenting a true, preferable alternative. You will need a plan to help you become a media-wise parent. With that, you can teach your teen to discern truth from lies, meaning from madness.

## Understand the Mission

I meet parents who are at their rope's end because they believe they have failed to protect their kids. One dad told me, "We've failed to protect him from the outside world. I've tried to keep him away from anything that would mislead him or promote impure thoughts in his mind or tempt him, but it hasn't worked."

I appreciate the pain this father is experiencing. But his concern points to what I believe is an error. If parents feel that their sole mission is to protect their teens from the world, they will always fail. Here's why.

First, we live in a fallen world. Sin is rampant. Unless you plan to keep your teen hidden away in the basement, you'll never completely isolate her from the world. One day you'll have to let her out.

Second, even if you unplugged the television, smashed your teen's cell phone, set the computer on fire, destroyed his iPad, and unsubscribed from Netflix, your teen would still be affected by the media's influence.

Third, your mission is not to hide the world from your teen; rather, it is to help her filter the messages of the world through a God-focused lens. Jesus didn't run from the world; He went to the world. He lived in it, teaching us how to see and do life from His perspective. You need to teach your child discernment, which is the ability to distinguish good from evil, to categorize what's helpful and what's harmful, and to make decisions that lead to a life of walking with the Lord regardless of the path taken by the world.

How do you do all that? It's important to hear what this generation is saying. When you know what your teen's needs are, you can help him succeed.

## Educate Yourself

We must become students of our teens' lives. Staying aware of all that is important to your child isn't easy, but it's necessary. In order to help your teen live wisely in an ever-changing world, you need to study and understand adolescent subculture. To help you get started, answer these questions:

- What is your teen's favorite song?
- What video game does she play most?
- What are the last four movies he watched?
- What concert does she want to attend next?
- What is the number one teen series on Netflix?

Your answers indicate how aware you are of your kid's life. I am not saying you have to watch every movie and television show and know the lyrics to every popular song, but you must not close yourself off from the teen world. By taking a few extra minutes each day, you can gain greater insight into the messages that compete for your teen's attention. Then you can help him discern what he hears, watches, and downloads. To do that, you need to ask the right questions. I rarely let a week go by without asking my daughters these questions:

- What songs are you listening to?
- What's the newest app you're using? (I also approve each app they download.)
- Which artist is the new thing right now?
- What are you watching?

I learn a lot simply by asking. If you haven't been asking questions, you need to start. This doesn't make you a snoop or a nag; it makes you a good parent. And it might help you learn a little about pop culture.

## Get Social

It takes time, but I monitor all the social media my daughters use. If your teen is on Facebook, Twitter, Instagram, or Snapchat, you need to be on the same social media platforms. As parents, we should view our kids' pages, posts, tweets, pins, and streaks and talk with them regularly about their accounts and who they follow. All this is necessary so we can help our families surf safely and use social media wisely. (In the next chapter you'll find tips on what you can do to teach your teen to be mature with mobile devices.)

## Use the Apps She Uses

One way Amy and I stay connected with our girls and remain media savvy is by using the apps they use. Not only does this keep us up to date on teen culture, but it also makes it easier to discuss photos, news, and the arts with our daughters. Our older daughter, Bailey, loves sports. She has the WatchESPN app, which pushes notifications to her with the latest scores, trends, and news in sports. I have the app too, so I get the same notifications. This makes it easy for us to discuss the playoffs, which player was traded, and other sports highlights. Brynnan, Bailey, and I all have the Grow On devotional app, which sends a short devotional to our phones each day. We often talk about the app's content, which consists of biblical topics and verses of Scripture. Using the apps my girls use gives me another opportunity to keep up with what's important to them.

## Start Streaming Music and Discuss Discernment

Apple Music, Amazon Music, iHeartRadio, and Spotify are a few of the music-streaming services. Amy and I subscribe to a music-streaming service because we love music. Having access to music libraries enables us to keep track of favorite artists and songs, and it inspires family dance-off moments in our living room. The service is not cheap, but we have decided to spend the money, believing the payoff is greater than the cost. Having music that we can share gives us another opportunity to connect with our girls about something that is important to them.

However, it's equally important to help your teen discern whether he should listen to particular artists or songs. I recently did a quick search of top albums on iTunes. Half the top albums have the "explicit" notification (the red *E* next to the name of the album). You should be aware of the music your teen is downloading or streaming.

A good rule of thumb is to avoid drawing battle lines based on your own musical tastes. Lyrics, not musical genres, are what's important. Research the bands and artists your teen likes. Google Play, iTunes, and just about any music-streaming service offer ratings and reviews, making it easy to research song lyrics. Do your research and then talk with her about it. Lead her in making wise decisions about music choices.

First Corinthians 10:31 offers great advice that can help when deciding what music to enjoy: "Whether you eat or drink or whatever you do, do it all for the glory of God." You can illuminate the facts about the music, and you can decide what is and isn't allowed in your home and on the devices your teen uses.

### Know What He Is Reading

Teens still read magazines.[1] Periodically pick up several teen magazines and look through them. Read them to learn about the culture. Look at the advertisements. Identify the worldview being depicted. If your teen is up for it, have him browse through a couple of magazines with you. Ask him about a particular article or advertisement. Find out how he feels it aligns (or doesn't align) with Scripture. This can be a great conversation starter to discuss fashion, sexual boundaries, and more. If your teen enjoys reading books, try reading and discussing any popular fiction or nonfiction books. This exercise is another opportunity to teach him how to navigate the world with wisdom and discernment.

## Enjoy Movies While Setting Wise Boundaries

Sunday is our family's regular Netflix-and-popcorn night. I hope you also have a family night that you work hard to protect. It could involve your family's favorite television shows, movies, or games, with your snack of choice.

If you have a Netflix subscription, you might be surprised to learn what type of content your family has ready access to. Netflix allows you to set up additional users, allowing each family member to utilize the service. You can check the viewing history of each user. I recently found more than twenty movies under the independent and international genres that I would label as porn. Several movies highlighted gay relationships and included same-sex nude love scenes. I found three that emphasized bondage and S&M.

Set up the parental controls that are included with a Netflix subscription. Log in to netflix.com, choose the profile you want to manage, enter the username and password, and select parental controls. If you get stuck, search "How to set up Netflix parental controls" online.

Take inventory of your teen's viewing selections. Pay close attention to the behaviors modeled in each movie, particularly language, dating, sex, attitudes toward parents and God, and so on. As you and your teen discuss her viewing history, emphasize the need to watch with discernment. It's good to watch a movie with her and then talk about the worldview depicted and the spiritual significance, or lack thereof. Such an exercise can make for a great family night. It can also help her think about cultural messages and the importance of using discernment when making movie and entertainment choices.

### Go Surfing

Make the effort to become a student of teen culture. It's important to look for opportunities to learn about the latest trends and ideas that have the potential to shape your family's worldview. The next time you are online checking the scores of your favorite team or downloading the recipe for the best chocolate chip cookies on the planet, go to a search engine and enter phrases such as "top teen websites," "teen trends," or "most popular teen video games." Then do some research. Additionally, check out the many online networking communities available to teens. Ask your teen about his favorite websites. By surfing a few teen sites, you'll learn a lot about what he is absorbing online.

### Hang Out with Teens

Another great way to keep up with what's happening is to volunteer to help with activities or projects at your teen's school or at another location where adolescents congregate. Listen to what kids are saying to one another. Notice what they're wearing. Observe how they interact with teachers and other adults.

Another suggestion is to volunteer to go to a student conference, concert, field trip, mission trip, weekend conference, or summer camp as an adult chaperone and worker. Spend a weekend or even a week with teens and you're bound to learn a lot.

### Make a Contract

A contract can establish standards and boundaries within your home. Make an agreement with your teen that limits the time she watches television, plays video games, and listens to music. Also, set parameters that spell out what content is acceptable. Document any media restrictions you have established in the agreement. Give her a hand in creating the document, and then have her sign it at the bottom.

What's feasible in a contract? A contract might stipulate the following:

- **Length of time.** "You are allowed to watch TV or play video games for a total of two hours each school night (or three hours per day on weekends). You are allowed to watch two movies per week. You are allowed to be online until ten o'clock each night."

- **Acceptable content.** "You are allowed to watch movies rated G and PG. Movies rated PG-13 and R generally are not allowed, but we may make exceptions if you discuss the movie with us first. (Examples might include *The Passion of the Christ* and *Schindler's List,* which are rated R but may be worth watching.) You are allowed to play video games that are on our approved list."

- **Punishment.** "We will enforce the terms of the agreed-upon contract by revoking privileges or enacting any additional consequences we deem necessary."

To make the contract work, you will need to be creative in how you design it and flexible in how you implement it. If something isn't working, you may need to revise the contract. Once you have a workable contract, be consistent in making sure your teen adheres to its stipulations, with negative consequences built in. Make sure he understands that you will remove privileges if the contract is not adhered to.

## Remember You're the Parent

Your teen doesn't need you to be a friend. Never forget: be the parent, not the pal. I want my daughters to like me, and I do have wonderful relationships with them. But they need me to be their parent first. There will be days when my parenting decisions don't sit well with them. You have to love your child so much that you are okay when she doesn't like you.

## Create a Family Mission Statement

When it comes to navigating media madness, I find that one of the most helpful tools is a family mission statement. During your next family devotional night, have each family member write down issues and ideas that are important to him or her. Then discuss the pertinent issues and develop a family mission statement together. Each family member should agree on the shared mission statement. Select a verse or passage of Scripture to be a part of this statement.

Use your mission statement as a guide to help you handle issues, dilemmas, and arguments both at home and away from home. When facing a family crisis, strive to make sure the result aligns with the mission statement.

Check out what Sherie and Steve told me:

We attended your parenting conference several months ago and just wanted you to know the difference it has made in our home since we applied the techniques you suggested. At first we were a little skeptical. Our oldest is sixteen, and he is pretty set in his ways. But we were determined, as you encouraged, to do our part.

The first night of our family devo time, we asked each of our three children to write a mission statement that he or she would like the family to follow. The next week, we gave each of them time to read his or her statement. It was eye opening to listen to the requests and obvious needs of our children, both emotional and physical. As we have made it a priority to spend even more time talking together as a family, we realize that our kids do want more of us. Thank you for laying it out for us and pushing us as parents to do more.

## Equip Your Teen to Pursue God

You need to challenge your teen to pursue God and defend his faith. Since you and your spouse are the number one influences in your child's life, he will be more likely to embrace this challenge if you embrace it and demonstrate it at home. When you defend your faith and articulate your worldview, you are equipping him to do the same.

The secret to rising above the media madness is not just avoiding worldliness and sin, though we are called to do that. The only way we can win is to passionately pursue God, press into Him, and delight in Him. I talk about this in more depth in chapter 17.

As Christians, we know that everything else but God will leave us used up and empty. If you can help your teen understand this, you will be equipping her with the secret to the purpose of life. You know what the world doesn't know: we exist to know God, enjoy Him, and glorify Him. It's wonderfully uncomplicated. Pass this truth on to your child.

You may be anxious, even fearful, of the negative influences that surround your teen. Don't be. Yes, the dangers are real and the results can be devastating. However, learning about teen culture, continuing to address the issues with him, and living as a godly example will help him develop a worldview that is in tune with God's desires. If you still feel ill equipped, I invite you to join the Jeffrey Dean Ministries mailing list. Our ministry produces a newsletter that focuses on teen culture. Visit jeffreydean.com for more information.

Here's a great prayer (based on Ephesians 3:14–19) that you can pray for your teen as she encounters the media madness:

*Father,*

*I kneel before You and pray that out of Your glorious riches, You may strengthen my teen with power through Your Spirit in her inner being so that Christ may dwell in her heart through faith. I pray that my child, being rooted and established in love, may have power to grasp how wide and long and high and deep is the love of Christ and to know this love that surpasses knowledge—that she may be filled to the measure of all Your fullness. Amen.*

# Setting Healthy Boundaries for Cell Phone Usage

I recently asked eight high school students in a youth detention center about their lives. These kids looked as though they had it all together, so why were they under the authority of the department of juvenile justice? By the time our conversation was over, I was saddened and shocked to learn the reason for their incarceration. Not one of these teens would graduate with their friends. Instead, they would graduate in a small room on the campus of a regional youth detention center. All eight were there for the same reason: sexting.

Sexting is defined as "the sending of sexually explicit messages or images by cell phone."[1] Many teens I meet are sexting now or have in the past, or they know someone who is.

It can be easy to believe there isn't much you can do to influence the direction of your teen's use of mobile devices. Don't believe the lie. While there are benefits to mobile devices—such as the ability to keep tabs on family, stay current on the news, make video calls, do research, and call a towing service or 911—there are just as many dangers. You need to understand how to navigate the world teens access on their phones. As you do that, you should develop a strategy to help your teen become mobile mature. (Yes, much of the information in this chapter also applies to internet use.)

Some teens build a lifestyle around their mobile devices and social media. They have the ability to keep their parents in the dark about what they're doing. You may feel intimidated by this topic, but there is much you can do to help your teen hold his own against the mobile mania. Communication plays a critical role, so building trust and talking are excellent ways to start.

## The Truth About Our Digital World

No one remains a teenager forever. Eventually, every high school student has to enter the adult world. Each of them will compete against other candidates for scholarships, jobs, promotions, graduate school, internships, advanced training, and other opportunities. In all these areas and many others, your teen's digital lifestyle—including attitude, mind-set, habits, biases, and other characteristics—can come back to haunt her later on. We need to help our teens face the hard facts now, in time to head major problems off at the pass. Here are a few facts you may not know about the world of cell phones and other mobile devices.

### Your Teen Has a Digital Footprint

A digital footprint is the trail you leave behind when you do anything online. Every time you access social media, open your browser, upload and edit your photo galleries, manage subscriptions, input credit card information, upload videos, watch a video on YouTube, and do pretty much anything else on the internet, you leave a trace. Most students don't give it a second thought when they add their name (and often their photo) to apps, games, or websites, but they need to be fully aware.

If your teen hopes to attend college or get a job in his chosen field, he needs to be reminded of the digital trail that is there for the dean of admissions and the hiring manager to see.[2] Studies show that up to 70 percent of employers use social media to screen candidates.[3] Once your teen posts a photo online, there is no end to where the content can go. What he posts can make a powerful statement about his character. If he isn't careful, he might find this out the hard way. Pipl.com is a great resource for showing your child the digital footprint he already has made.

### Your Teen Is the Target Market

Corporations work hard to lure consumers, especially young consumers, to their products. When your teen makes a purchase or conducts a search using a mobile device, advertisers create a link between her and a product or service she might have an interest in. Data harvesting, retargeting, cookie sharing—terms that didn't even exist just a few years ago—are standard practices in the digital-marketing era. Every time she chats, tweets, posts, or searches things online, she most likely is inputting data that is documented, recorded, and used for selling products. Where is all that information about your child going? That's a good question.

### They *Know Where Your Teen Is*

Unless you disable the feature, many smartphone apps track your child's location. This is potentially an invasion of privacy, and it frequently happens without people knowing it. Apps that use location data can be helpful, such as for navigation and checking the weather. But if your teen allows any app to track his location, he also may be allowing that app to sell the location data. Some of the world's most popular apps do not work without being able to track the user's location. Many are loaded with covert marketing—basically, conversations between brands and users. It's important to know which apps are following your teen. It is also critical to know how to deactivate the apps.

### It's All Out There (and I Do Mean All)

Pornography sites are the most visited sites on the internet. Every second, 28,258 users watch porn via their phones or computers.[4] Pornhub, the top online porn site, registers on average 2.1 million views every hour,[5] and one out of every five mobile searches seeks out pornography.[6] As the writer of one article stated, "If it exists, there is a 'dirty' version based on it."[7] I've dedicated an entire chapter to the problem of pornography (see chapter 12).

Porn isn't the only danger. It is alarming that our teens carry around devices that enable them to access similar junk with only a few clicks. Do you know about Sex, Etc.? If not, you need to. Sex, Etc. is a popular site for middle school and high school students that offers teen-targeted relationship and sex-education help. On the site I found answers to questions such as these:

- Is it okay to date someone older than you?
- Which condom is the best?
- How do you deal with homophobic bullying?

In the "All About Condoms" section, I found an article titled "Anal Sex: From Stigma and Myths to Facts." The article provides the following advice: "Taking part in any sex act should always be safe and consensual—and you shouldn't feel ashamed of your desires!" The writer advises, "It can feel overwhelming to tell your partner what you want, especially when it's something like anal sex, which is often not discussed in general. But it's ideal to talk about anything new before trying it."[8] Several other articles offer detailed steps describing oral sex, masturbation alone or with a partner, and how to split a condom so you can use it to give oral sex to a girl while using protection.[9] This same site refers to abortion as a very safe procedure and mentions on several occasions that a second abortion is no big deal.[10] Planned Parenthood's website has quizzes and games that detail safe-sex practices, give advice on finding the right sexual partner, and more.[11]

## Device-Driven Social Apps

We discussed social media in the previous chapter, but we now need to focus on social apps, which allow users to subscribe and thus become your teen's "friend." And the "friends of friends" feature invites her to communicate within a limited community or with the world at large. While such apps can increase your teen's circle of friends, they also can increase exposure to people with less-than-honorable intentions. It is critical that you establish healthy guidelines when it comes to her use of apps and her participation in the online social scene. Here are some parameters you might want to consider:

- **Know user logins for all your teen's accounts.** I have a password manager app on all my devices. I use it to store the user logins and passwords for my entire family. If you aren't using a similar app, make sure you keep all your teen's login information in a secure place. Knowing the user logins allows you to log in to your child's accounts and monitor his social media presence.

- **Know your teen's friends.** You probably know who your child spends time with at school. You also should know who she spends time with online. One of the rules you need to establish is that you have full access to her social media connections.

- **Monitor your teen's pics and streaks.** Know what images he is posting. This is why it's important for you to use all the apps your teen uses and be one of his social media friends on each app.

- **Remind your teen that once she hits Send, there is no end.** The things she posts in apps, websites, and streaks can never be erased. They always will remain searchable. I encourage my girls to pause before hitting Send so they can ask themselves, *Could this post negatively affect my future?*

- **Limit your teen's usage.** Just as you have limits on TV time and video games, you need to set parameters when it comes to your child's mobile device use. Establish guidelines for phone use in the bedroom (for example, only after homework is complete). The most important rule to enforce is that cell phones should never be used while driving.

- **School rules rule.** Amy and I expect our daughters to never walk out of school looking at their phones. We want them to see other people, communicate with others, and otherwise not be distracted. We also require they follow the mobile device rules their teachers establish in the classroom and on campus.

- **Your teen learns by watching you.** If you are updating your social media accounts or tweeting every opportunity you get, you are setting a usage precedent that he will likely follow.

## Become Smartphone Savvy

A friend told me, "My daughter spends more time on the phone than she does talking to us." Teens aren't the only ones who give in to addictive cell phone behavior. I have a number of adult friends who are way too consumed with their devices. But teens, to a greater degree than adults, have learned to communicate using their thumbs. It is up to you to establish rules, draw up a contract, and model the lifestyle you want your child to adopt. You can download a free mobile device contract at jeffrey dean.com.

If your teen (or any child in your family, regardless of age) spends time online, the principles in your contract will be helpful in establishing healthy online habits for your family. Spell out your expectations and then live by them. The contract is a crucial part of your attempt to safeguard your teen's mobile and online life. But you can't leave it at that. Here are several other critical things to know.

### Beware the New Social Flirt

Think about the risky things you did as a teen. Now think about sexting in the same context. Many teens consider sexting a normal part of teen culture. Teens do it to flirt, out of rebellion or sexual curiosity, in an attempt to gain a sense of significance, in the pursuit of love, or because of peer pressure.

If you won't talk to your teen about the dangers of sexting, who will? She needs to know that the sexting laws in most parts of the country define this widespread teenage practice as a crime. If you sent it, you committed a crime. If you received it and didn't immediately delete it, you, too, committed a crime. As you discuss this critical issue with your teen, ask questions such as these:

- If someone pressures you to send a sext, how will you respond?
- Regardless of the legal ramifications, how can sexting damage your spiritual life?
- If you know someone who has sent a sext, why do you believe he or she did so?
- If you send a sext and the relationship ends, how will you feel about those photos still being out there?

Teens who say that their parents discuss sexting with them are less likely to sext.[12] Be willing to go there.

## Consider a Keylogger

Keylogger software logs every key pressed on the keyboard of your mobile device or computer. It can capture messages, passwords, downloads, images, and videos sent. Your teen can accidentally stumble onto something he was not looking for, and keylogger software can help you protect him by notifying you that he has wandered into dangerous territory. Of course, this may not prevent him from viewing the content at that specific moment. But the knowledge of what has happened can kick-start a candid conversation about what to do if and when a situation like this arises again. Keep in mind that this software also invites you into your teen's private conversations. You should weigh the pros and cons before using it.

Keylogger software collects keyboard and mobile device data such as

- phone location
- amount of time your teen spends on her computer
- most frequently visited apps and websites
- a record of every keystroke
- most-used contacts on his phone
- a log of all calls, texts, chats, emails, and Skype

This software includes red-flag notifications. You can activate these in the admin setup section and receive notifications for words, phone numbers, and websites you deem potentially dangerous. If you flag words such as *suicide, school shootings,* and *porn,* you will receive a notification immediately if these words are used on the logged device. The red flag can be important to alert you to potentially harmful content, communication your teen might be having with someone she should not be talking to, or evidence that she might be searching for ways to harm herself or others.

## Check Search History

After attending one of our parenting events, a father told me he went home to check his teen's recent online activity. On the home computer he found there was no search history available. "I knew immediately that someone was trying to hide something," he said, "so we had a family meeting."

A computer's browser history can be easily erased. If you find that the history for your teen's mobile device or computer has been cleaned out, it's probably time for a family conversation. Let him know that you will consistently check his online life. This does not make you a nag or intrusive parent; it makes you a good parent.

### Take Extreme Measures When Necessary

If you believe that your teen is hiding something, you need to do something now, not later. You must be willing to take extreme measures when necessary to protect her. Remind her that using a mobile device or a laptop is a privilege that can be taken away.

### Communicate

Ask questions. Make it clear that you will remain proactive in communicating with your teen about his online and cell phone habits. Remember, it is never too late to begin to communicate.

## It All Begins with You

You have a responsibility to teach your child how powerfully addictive mobile devices can be. I attended a high school graduation ceremony and watched a father miss his daughter walking across the stage to receive her diploma. He was too preoccupied with his cell phone. He missed an important moment in his daughter's life that he can never retrieve. I hope she didn't notice.

Whenever I am on my phone, I am telling my wife and daughters that my phone is more important in that moment than they are. We have to be determined not to let our phones supersede critical moments with our kids. Here is a simple and necessary rule: everyone (including you) puts the phones away at dinner. Dinnertime can be the best opportunity to focus on your family and learn what's going on in everyone's life.

Let your teen see you watching as she plays lacrosse, performs with the school choir, or shows her paintings in the school art exhibit. Do not scroll through your Facebook timeline instead. When helping her study or work on a project, leave your phone in another room. My younger daughter learns best when I help her focus on the task at hand. My phone can be a distraction.

I have found that the drive home from school often is the time when my daughters talk most about their day. School is fresh in their minds, they are glad to be done for the day, and there is often something they have been waiting to tell me. Because I honor them and value this time, my phone is inaccessible during our commute.

We have made it clear that our daughters should not take their phones to bed. We encourage them instead to have a devotional time with God just before they fall asleep. Amy and I try to do the same thing. I don't want my girls to see that the last thing I focus on at the end of the day is my phone.

Help point your teen back to Scripture. Matthew 10:16 reads, "I am sending you out like sheep among wolves. Therefore be as shrewd as snakes and as innocent as doves." Suggest that your child make this verse his life scripture when it comes to navigating the digital world. The likelihood of your teen's falling prey to a sexual predator may be minimal. The greater message is to encourage him to live in a way that honors God, especially when it comes to cell phone use.

Your teen's online life either honors God or dishonors Him. Everything she tweets, posts, searches, and sends lets the world know who she lives for. Work to instill in your teen a mobile-mature lifestyle that proclaims, "Above all, I am a follower of Christ."

# What to Do About Pornography

heard the following from a twenty-seven-year-old man who attended a presentation I gave at a large church:

> I first viewed porn in my bedroom when I was in seventh grade. At first it was a casual thing. It eventually became an everyday thing. By the time I graduated from college, it was a full-blown addiction. It wasn't until I had been married several years and had a baby girl that anyone found out about my secret. By then it had gotten so bad that my wife was devastated. Right now we aren't divorced, but we have separated. I am hopeful that we can work it out. She's angry, and I understand her anger. I had this eleven-year secret that I never told anyone about. I wish I'd had someone to talk to about my addiction. I've lost jobs, money, my reputation, and, most tragic of all, potentially my marriage.

Pornography can threaten to destroy just about anyone at any age. The difference between this man's story and your teen's story is *you*. You can make all the difference by beginning a conversation about pornography now. The difference between people who live as porn addicts and those who find freedom is someone who is willing to take the addict in hand and walk the journey with her.

As stated in chapter 11, one in five mobile device internet searches is aimed at finding pornography. The revenue of the online pornography industry in the United States has topped $3 billion annually.[1] And it's only a click away. Even when you're not looking for it, porn can find you. Once you've downloaded it into your mind's hard drive, the harmful images can keep replaying over and over.

For some people porn seems to be no big deal. I talked backstage with a group of college students at a Christian conference. We spoke candidly about college life, dating, and purity. Read what they said about porn:

- "I view porn more than I'm willing to admit. It's almost weekly." (Hailey, twenty)
- "It's so easy to see. I've even watched porn while in class." (Josh, nineteen)
- "Even as a Christ follower, I find it very hard to say no." (Pete, twenty-one)

Teens who struggle with pornography are not oddball, sadistic, perverted teens. Instead, most are honor-roll, churchgoing, love-their-parents, striving-to-live-for-Jesus teens. I talk with just as many girls as I do guys about their porn-viewing habits. Sixty-four percent of young people between the ages of thirteen and twenty-four actively seek out pornography at least weekly.[2] Thirty-two percent of teens admit to looking at online porn. Of these, 43 percent do so on a weekly basis.[3]

I often meet adults who can't fathom how someone can get caught up in such filth. Even when some parents realize their son or daughter is addicted to porn, the Enemy often has won the fight by convincing the parents they are ill equipped to help their teen. But the struggle with pornography isn't different from the struggle with any other sin: Satan presents us with dangerous, cleverly packaged lies that look inviting. We are tempted, and temptation gives birth to sin.

Sin affects us all. Romans 3:23 reminds us that "all have sinned and fall short of the glory of God." If your teen struggles with porn, make it clear that you understand the struggle because you battle sin in your own life. Most importantly, communicate that your teen is not alone. Maybe you yourself have been tempted to view porn. If so, you can share in a personal way what that struggle has been like and how you have achieved victory.

Certainly, we can't be passive about the problem. The question isn't "Will my teen view pornography?" Rather, the question is "When will it happen?" The necessary follow-up question should be "How far am I willing to go to help protect my teen from pornography?"

Hebrews 12:1 tells us to "throw off everything that hinders and the sin that so easily entangles." Ephesians 5:3 warns that we should be free of "even a hint of sexual immorality, or of any kind of impurity, or of greed, because these are improper for God's holy people." Helping your teen avoid or overcome porn addiction is one of the most important responsibilities you have. Let's talk more about what you're up against.

## In Just One Click

A college sophomore told me he had gotten hooked on internet porn when he was in high school. During his senior year he was required to write a term paper on human anatomy. One afternoon he was online, reading about the study of the human body. Clicking on a link in search of images of the female anatomy, a porn site appeared. He quickly left the site. But the more he sat in front of his computer, the more he thought about the images. He found himself going back again and again. Thus began a dark journey that lasted most of his senior year of high school.

An endless number of teens have told me they receive inappropriate spam mail—unsolicited email that often leads to a website, usually pornographic. Sometimes the initial spam messages appear innocuous, such as an invitation to check out a magazine subscription or some cartoons or jokes. Sometimes the advertisements are a bit racier.

You may have received such spam. I got one of these messages on my cell phone. It said, "Hey, sexy, I saw your profile online and want to send you a few pics of me. Click this link and let's get to know each other." Whoever sent this spam might have obtained my email address from a program that crawls the internet in search of email addresses. Or my address may have been sold to a company. Or it may have been obtained from a program that searches for names on the internet and creates plausible email addresses from the original names, hoping that one in a thousand will hit the mark.

Pornography seeks and destroys. It's imperative that you realize it can be right in front of your teen in just one click.

## The Trouble with Porn

Isn't this just a phase that all teens go through, particularly boys? Nothing could be further from the truth. The more your teen views porn, the more his view of the opposite sex will change. Eventually, your teen will stop seeing people as God sees them and begin seeing them merely as a means to fulfill his desires. Pornography turns other people into objects of lust.

If your teen dates and is viewing porn, it will be only a matter of time before she becomes more physical with her dating partner. The fantasy world she is watching will keep pushing to turn itself into reality. Your teen will be tempted to use people to fulfill personal lust. And as she tries to act out the sexual behavior viewed online, the perceived need for self-gratification will damage not only her relationships during her dating years but also her relationship with a future mate.

As your teen dives more deeply into the world of porn, his character will begin to be eroded, even destroyed. We read in Galatians 6:8, "Who-ever sows to please their flesh, from the flesh will reap destruction." Teens might believe they can casually check out porn and still live within God's will. If so, they are being fooled. If they sow to please their lust, destruc-tion is soon to follow.

As your teen hands over one area of her life to Satan, it will be only a matter of time before the Enemy demands other areas as well. Here are warning signs that may signal that your teen is viewing porn:

- secretiveness when using the computer or a smartphone
- erased password and browser history
- diminished interest in socializing with friends
- consistent time spent alone in the bedroom or bathroom with the door locked
- decreased interest in school and extracurricular activities
- excessive interest in dating

## What You Can Do

If your teen is into porn, you don't have time to waste. With every look and every image, he is going deeper into darkness. The Enemy wants you to feel guilty. He wants you to question how this could have happened to your teen. He will work overtime to convince you that you have failed miserably.

Just this week I had lunch with a father of four. He told me, "I feel as though I've blown it. We just found out Thomas is viewing porn. We are devastated. We don't know how we missed it, but we did. I thought I was doing everything right, but Thomas still got caught up in this stuff."

This can happen to anyone's kid. You can do everything right and still have a child who gets, as my friend put it, "caught up in this stuff." You can't control everything your child does. There will be times when she will choose to do wrong. It's in this moment that Satan wants you to believe that you're the worst parent ever. This is when you have to remind yourself that Satan is a liar.

No matter what happened prior to this point, you can help your teen break free. He does not have to continue down this degrading path. We read in 1 John 4:4, "Little children, you are from God and have overcome them, for he who is in you is greater than he who is in the world" (ESV). God can bring your child out of this place of darkness.

I have yet to counsel a teen struggling with porn who desired to continue struggling. Nobody wants to be a slave to sin and remain on the road to destruction. Yet many who want to escape from bondage have little knowledge of how to overcome its grip. If your teen struggles with porn, she needs your help. Here are ten steps to help your child find freedom.

## 1. Realize That Sexual Cravings Are Normal

We all have sexual cravings. Acknowledging this helps answer the question "How did my teen get addicted to porn?" When teens see porn for the first time, it might shock them, upset them, or make them feel guilty. However, it also will awaken their sexual drives while urging them to repeat the experience. Porn is a powerful influencer. When teens see it, a new awareness ignites in them at a vulnerable stage of development.

Dopamine is a neurotransmitter that is involved in many different pathways in our brains. It often is identified as the "molecule behind all our most sinful behavior and secret cravings. . . . Really, dopamine is signaling feedback for predicted rewards."[4] It is an important driver of sexual desire and also increases essential survival behavior, such as eating and protecting ourselves from excessive heat or cold. When your teen looks at porn, it triggers an overwhelming amount of dopamine, which makes the impulse to look and keep looking increasingly hard to resist.

## 2. Don't Dance Around the Problem

If you don't talk with your teen about porn, who will? Many parents talk about porn and sexuality, but only indirectly. Don't dance around the issue. Share the specific effects porn has on a person's life. Even if you think your teen is not yet involved with porn, don't wait to have this talk. If he spends time online, it is inevitable that he will be exposed to porn. If you have caught him viewing porn, at first he may deny that the struggle exists or try to minimize its effects. It is critical that you explain how hard Satan works to get people hooked. What an awesome moment this can be to strengthen your relationship with your teen and help him see you as someone who longs to protect him from harm.

## 3. Love the Teen; Hate the Sin

As you implement each of these steps, remind your teen that you love her and that your love will never change. She needs to know that although you disagree with her actions, you want to help her defeat this addiction and be restored to a pure life. Brian, age seventeen, told me, "I did what you suggested I should do and told my parents. I thought they would hate me. They were disappointed in me but also told me they were glad I came to them. It felt so good to finally come clean, and knowing they still love me made all the difference in the world."

I encourage you to communicate to your teen every day that regardless of behavior, you love him. Knowing that your love remains strong will empower him as he works to find freedom.

## 4. Understand That a Promise Isn't Enough

If you catch your teen in the act of watching porn, her initial response may be to quickly apologize, plead for your forgiveness, and promise never to do it again. Though her desire to repent may be genuine, it may be only a matter of time before the addiction wins again. For a teen struggling with porn, a promise to change isn't enough. You need to help her make the promise a reality.

## 5. Help Your Teen Acknowledge, Be Specific, and Confess

God is aware of every image in your teen's mind, but He still loves him. You have a critical responsibility, second only to God's, to help your child reconcile the darkness of his life and take the steps necessary to renew a relationship with God. Jeremiah 29:11 says that the Lord has a plan for each of us, a plan to prosper us and to give us hope and a future. This plan often begins with confession. In 1 John 1:9 we read, "If we confess our sins, he will forgive our sins, because we can trust God to do what is right. He will cleanse us from all the wrongs we have done" (NCV).

Lead your teen through these confession steps. Encourage her to be completely honest with God as she confesses mistakes and receives God's forgiveness.

- **Acknowledge the sin.** God can handle the truth. "Come to me, all you who are weary and burdened, and I will give you rest. Take my yoke upon you and learn from me, for I am gentle and humble in heart, and you will find rest for your souls. For my yoke is easy and my burden is light" (Matthew 11:28–30).
- **Be specific.** God wants us to be as specific as we can be about our sins. "We have sinned and done wrong. We have been wicked and turned against you, your commands, and your laws. . . . Lord, you are good and right, but we are full of shame today. . . . But, Lord our God, you show us mercy and forgive us even though we have turned against you" (Daniel 9:5, 7, 9, NCV).
- **Confess.** God offers forgiveness no matter what.

I acknowledged my sin to you,
>   and I did not cover my iniquity;
I said, "I will confess my transgressions to the LORD,"
>   and you forgave the iniquity of my sin . . . .

You are a hiding place for me;
>   you preserve me from trouble;
>   you surround me with shouts of deliverance.
>       (Psalm 32:5, 7, ESV)

## 6. Take Inventory and Remove Temptation

Your teen must be willing to submit his future choices, actions, and thoughts to God. This could mean that for a while he commits to avoiding any form of entertainment that may activate a desire for more porn consumption. Consider the types of media outlets your teen has access to at home. These could include cable television, Netflix, Hulu, various music platforms, and the internet. Which of these might tempt him to sin? Consider what he watches and listens to. What influences do these media messages have?

If you suspect or know that your teen struggles with porn, remove the source from your home immediately. If the source is a computer, place it in a high-traffic area and ensure that she never has access to it unless you are present. If the source is a television, it must go. If the source is a cell phone, it must go. In addition, never let your teen keep a computer or cell phone in her room overnight. No questions, no rationalizing.

This is war. You can't expect to defeat Satan if you invite him into your home. Of course, such a purge will not eliminate access to all the porn in the world. But by removing the immediate sources, you will send a strong message to your child that you are prepared to take extreme measures to break the bondage.

## 7. Develop a Strategy

It is unrealistic to think that just because you remove sources of temptation from the home, your teen will never again be tempted to use porn. So develop a strategy to help him no matter where he is. There is no one-size-fits-all strategy. I recommend that you and your spouse (if you're married) outline a game plan before discussing it with your teen. The game plan should include, but not be limited to, the following:

- **Set up a regular daily routine.** Your teen needs to see the importance of a disciplined, routine schedule. This does not mean completely isolating her from daily activities, hobbies, and interests; it means setting boundaries on what she is allowed to do, which helps develop a greater sense of security. Keep her schedule full so her mind remains occupied. Chores, sports, a part-time job, and volunteering can be appropriate outlets.

- **Approve friendships.** Your teen's friends play a huge role in his decision-making. Teens often tell me that they view porn while at a friend's house. Teach your teen how to refuse a friend's invitation to view porn. Choosing friends who are in line with God's will for his life is a critical step to overcoming the temptation to check out porn. We read in 1 Corinthians 15:33, "Bad company corrupts good character." It is essential that he chooses friends who push him toward God rather than away from Him. Let your teen know you want open communication about who his friends are and where his time is spent.

- **Kill the lies.** Satan often wins when he wins in your teen's mind. Communicate to your child that Satan will work to sell lies such as "What's the big deal? It's just a picture of a naked person. Besides, looking at porn is a lot better than

sleeping with someone." Satan's lies might also take the form
of "You are so good in every other area of life. This is just
your one failing." Statements such as "No one is going to
know. And what harm will really come from it?" or "I
deserve this. I've had a really tough week" indicate that
your teen has begun to believe Satan's lies and is rationalizing her behavior.

- **Keep talking.** If your teen has been checking out porn for
  some time, it is probable that he will experience setbacks
  while working to resist the temptation and to walk in purity.
  Evil forces will try to drive harmful desires more deeply into
  his mind. The best way to combat this is to communicate
  often with him. Regularly ask questions such as "How are
  you feeling about your struggle?" or "Have you had any
  setbacks?" or "What's going on in your head?" Let him see
  that you are serious about walking every step of the way
  with him, no matter how long it takes.

- **Set a good example.** Let your teen see that you reject any
  sexualized messages on television and in the movies you
  watch. Change the channel or mute the sound during
  commercials that use sex to sell. When you do this, seize
  the opportunity to talk about the message in the movie
  or the commercial. Ask questions such as "What is that
  commercial saying about women?" or "Why do you think
  Hollywood seems to go out of its way to get sex and nudity
  into movies?"

- **Establish goals.** Help your teen develop a set of goals to
  achieve, and celebrate together when she makes significant
  progress. Give her additional freedom as she proves
  trustworthy.

## 8. Prioritize Scripture

A key to overcoming a porn addiction rests in your teen's commitment to spending consistent time in God's Word. Help him find Scripture verses to memorize. Display these verses throughout your home. Write them on note cards and drop them in his lunch box or backpack. Laminate a card with a personal note from you along with a verse and put it in your son's wallet or your daughter's purse. Hang verses on your teen's bathroom mirror.

I have long challenged students across the country to find specific verses or passages of Scripture that will help in their struggles. Remember how Jesus responded to the temptation He faced from Satan? Three times He was tempted, and three times He responded by quoting Scripture. Keeping the Word in front of your teen will help her resist sin. Psalm 119:9 promises you and her, "How can a young person stay on the path of purity? By living according to your word."

## 9. Pray Like Crazy

Prayer is the greatest strategy you can implement. Pray specifically. Pray Scripture. Pray for your teen. Pray *with* your teen. Pray over your teen. Prayer is your source of strength when the fight takes you into the eleventh round. Prayer is your greatest weapon against Satan's ploys to get him to take a bite of the forbidden fruit.

## 10. Never Give Up

If you are feeling hopeless, find hope in this: God hasn't given up on your teen. He won't ever throw in the towel. He is committed all the way to you and her. Find your hope in Him, and when all else seems hopeless, hold fast to Isaiah 40:31: "Those who hope in the LORD will renew their strength. They will soar on wings like eagles; they will run and not grow weary, they will walk and not be faint."

# Talking with Your Teen About Dating

A teenager named Jenna sent me this email in response to my book *This Is Me:*

> I have read the chapter on dating twice. Every word you said reminded me that I don't have to settle when it comes to who I date. My parents have never really been there for me, so I've had to navigate all of this on my own. Many guys are only interested in one thing when they ask you out. I've found that out the hard way. Thank you for reminding me that I don't have to be that girl anymore. I love what you said: "Waiting patiently for the right guy makes you smart—and makes God proud." That's the person I'm trying to be now—smart!

I hear from more and more teens who no longer want to settle when it comes to dating. Relativism permeates our culture, sending a tragic message that there is no such thing as absolute right and wrong. The line between what's acceptable and what's not has become increasingly blurred.

Turn on a television or browse through a teen magazine and you'll see that everyone has an opinion to give your teen about dating. Reality TV depicts dating as a game that can be won by the last contestant standing. Magazine ads insist that teen girls should use their bodies to attract attention. Commercials often depict women as ornaments on display to entice the male eye. Teens are bombarded with titillating messages that showcase male and female interaction as lustful and uncontrollable. A generation of teens is accepting the notion that anything goes. Accordingly, a lot of teens struggle in their dating lives.

Helping your teen in this area requires that you be all in. Unfortunately, most parents I talk to have no strategy in place to help guide and guard their teens through the dating years. Do you? Part of your role is to help your teen craft a dating strategy. After countless conversations with teens, I'm convinced that dating is their number one source of struggle and heartbreak.

Most teens tell me that their parents never talk to them about dating. That means most teens with no experience, no guidance, and no plan in place are making critical decisions on their own. How are teens going to answer the following questions wisely?

- Is this person datable?
- Is it okay to get into a car with someone my parents don't know?
- What will I do if there is alcohol at a party?
- What if someone invites me over when no parents are home?
- How do I respond if I receive a sext?
- What do I do if I feel threatened with physical violence?
- What is my plan of action if someone I'm with starts smoking, doing drugs, or juuling?[1]
- Is it really a big deal if my date wants to hook up?
- Should we kiss on the first date, the tenth date, or never?

- What if my date isn't a Christian? Does that even matter?
- How am I supposed to feel about myself if I can't get a date?

These are just a few of the big questions teens have about dating. They want the answers to these questions and more, whether they realize it or not. Dating can be a wonderful time for your teen to develop healthy, God-centered relationships. Dating also can help him develop independence and demonstrate trustworthiness.

## Develop a Workable Plan

When you believe the time is right for your teen to begin dating, your goal is to help her develop habits that make dating fun and safe while honoring God. So settle in and let's develop a strategy that works for you *and* your teen.

### Ask the Right Questions

We teach our teens to answer the *why* and *what* questions in many areas of life, including integrity, responsibility, and accountability. Encouraging our kids to aspire to the same high standards in the area of dating is just as important. For instance:

- Why date?
- Why do you want to date this particular person?
- What do you hope to gain by dating?
- What kind of person would you never date?

Help your teen ask the right questions. Then help him form a clearly articulated answer for each question. Dating shouldn't be something he does merely to fill a void in his calendar. Getting your teen into the rhythm of answering questions such as these will teach him how to be intentional about dating while establishing healthy and realistic boundaries.

## Encourage Going Solo

I know a girl who seems to have everything going for her. She is beautiful, smart, athletic, and godly. Yet she is single. One day she'll find a wonderful partner. But for now, she's cool with going solo. She told me, "Why rush it? I'm enjoying high school, sports, and spending time with my friends. Dating usually just confuses everything, and I am in no hurry for that."

Your teen doesn't have to date just because she is a teenager. Choosing not to date frees a teen to focus on grades, sports, family, and much more.

I'm often asked how old teens should be before they start dating. It's not about their age but about their level of maturity. Not every teen has to date, nor is every one ready to date. It's okay to encourage yours to hold off from dating. Teens need to know that they aren't losers if they're single.

In a previous book I wrote about Brad, a guy other guys wanted to be and every girl wanted to date. Good looks, good grades, cool car—he had it all. But Brad wasn't concerned with dating. He told me, "I can't wait to meet the girl I'll spend the rest of my life with. But until then, I'd rather skip all the hassle and temptation of dating. I'm having a blast playing ball, hanging with friends, and just being single."

Some teens believe they have to date because everyone else does. But it's okay not to date. In fact, choosing not to date frees a teen from dating drama and provides a greater sense of focus for developing a strong personality, life skills, and a God-centered worldview.

## Emphasize Communication

Jessica, age sixteen, recently emailed me and said, "My mom is okay with me dating. I have been in only one serious relationship this year, but there are a lot of questions and things I'm confused about. My mom has never really talked to me about guys or any of that stuff. I'm thankful she isn't too strict, but I also know I don't have it all figured out. Should I approach my mom and invite her into my personal life? Or should I just keep things the way they are and not risk having her involvement?"

Jessica longs for her mom's input. A mom told me, "I don't push myself on my son, but I let him know that I am here if and when he wants to talk. And talk is exactly what he has started doing. Early on in his dating years, he didn't tell me a lot. But as he's gotten older, I think he's come to understand that I am safe. We now talk openly about it all, and our relationship is stronger because of it."

Isn't this what we all desire—to have a close connection with our teens? Let your teen know that you'll talk about any subject. He needs your help in understanding what should and should not happen on a date. Talk to him about dating. Ask questions. Encourage him to tell you what's happening.

A great starting point is for you to clearly communicate your expectations. Tell your teen that you always want to know where she is, whom she is with, and what time she will be home. Rules don't make you a legalistic parent; they make you a good parent.

If your teen is already dating, then introducing dating guidelines may not sit well with him. Tell him why you want to be more involved. Explain that you want to help him avoid the heartache that results from making wrong choices. Once your teen leaves the house, there is no guarantee he will abide by your wishes, but try to communicate your desire to be in the know when it comes to his dating experiences.

### Prioritize God

God wants to be involved in every aspect of your child's life. Encouraging her to walk closely with the Lord is essential. To have a dating life that pleases God, she must commit to communicate with God and seek His will.

I am confident that as your child commits time to prayer, reading the Bible, and fellowshipping with people who do the same, God will guide him. Psalm 1:1–2 reads, "Happy are those who don't listen to the wicked, who don't go where sinners go, who don't do what evil people do. They love the LORD's teachings, and they think about those teachings day and night" (NCV). Our joy comes from reading and meditating on the Bible.

These practices also will remind your teen that her value and significance are found not in a dating relationship but rather in a committed relationship with Jesus Christ. As she develops a deeper relationship with Christ, her sense of security will reflect God's plan and purpose.

A college student told me, "I am experiencing firsthand the benefit of having applied the 'time in the Word' principle. I want you to know this discipline has paid off. The more I have been in the Word, the more confidence I have developed in my walk with God. Now that I am in college, I realize that my degree, social status, and future girlfriend do not define me. God does. I'm willing to patiently wait for the right girl who also desires to love God more than anything. Thank you for pushing us to get our priorities right with God."

The decision to prioritize God above all else will give your teen the secure identity, purpose, and meaning that are found only in Him.

### Talk About Abuse

A *U.S. News & World Report* article stated, "Each year, approximately 1.5 million high school students nationwide will experience dating abuse. . . . 1 in 10 high school students who dated someone in the past 12 months reported being slapped or purposefully hit and physically hurt by a romantic partner. . . . According to the Centers for Disease Control and Prevention, 23 percent of females and 14 percent of males first experienced dating abuse between the ages of 11 and 17 years."[2]

A large number of students have told me they have been victims of dating violence. Many who experience emotional, psychological, or sexual abuse never tell anyone. According to a study in the *Journal of Adolescent Health,* 55 percent of parents say they have spoken with their child about teen dating violence.[3] Have you?

I believe that extreme video games and the accessibility of graphic porn that frequently portrays sadism and masochism contribute to the increase in dating violence. Signs that your teen may be in an abusive relationship include declining grades, withdrawing from relationships and former interests, being secretive or sneaky, and a decline in self-care. Tell your teen that no one ever has the right to abuse him in any way.

## Model Good Dating Etiquette

Dad, bring your preteen or teen along the next time you take your wife on a date. Use the occasion to help your child better understand what dating should be about. Seeing you opening doors for your wife, pulling out her chair, being respectful, complimenting her, and avoiding any unsafe environment will show sons and daughters alike what they should expect on a date. Daughters will see how they should be treated by a guy, and sons will know how to treat girls. What an excellent way for you to model what it means to respect and be respected by a date.

## Encourage Group Dates

Group dating allows teens to be with additional friends while on a date. As your teen shows that she is trustworthy, you can choose to give more dating freedom—in a group or otherwise.

Ideally, you set the restrictions for group dating. For instance, your teen can meet a date at a youth event where a youth pastor and other parents are present. Or you could drop him off at the mall or at a youth event to meet a date along with a group of friends. The options are limitless.

A great way to help teens who have never dated is to require that they date at home first. One father told me that whenever his daughter begins a new dating relationship, he requires her to spend the first three dates at home. This allows the parents to meet their daughter's new guy. If the girl does not mean enough to the new date for the guy to abide by the dad's dating rules, then he most likely is not the right one to date her.

## Define Who Is Datable

Here is a great question to ask your teen: "If you could design the person you want to spend the rest of your life with, what would the person be like?" A good follow-up question is "Consider the people you've dated or want to date. Do these people match up with your list? If not, why are you dating or wanting to date the person?"

A teen girl who spends time in God's Word will look for a godly young man who will respect her. Teens may worry that if they have such high standards, they'll never go out. It's true that maintaining high standards will shrink the pool of datable people. If teens choose to lower their standards, the number of potential dates will increase, but they may be dating people who are unworthy or unsuitable.

Setting high expectations can make teens feel as though they are missing out. But if they have to compromise to get a date, they're putting dating ahead of God—and nothing should come before Him. Everything around them reinforces the message that they *need* to have a boyfriend or girlfriend and that something's wrong with them if they don't. This might be the lie teens believe more than any other. Waiting patiently for the right person can be one of the hardest things to do. Look for ways to remind your teen that she will regret lowering her standards a lot more than going bowling with you on Friday night.

## Never Compromise on Faith

When a teen asks if it's all right to date someone who is not a Christian, I answer him or her with the following questions:

- Would you want to marry someone who doesn't believe in God, heaven, or hell?
- Would you want to marry someone who doesn't read the Bible, go to church, and pray?
- Would you want to marry someone who wouldn't instill in your children godly character or teach them to pray, go to church, and read the Bible?

I hope the answer to these questions for you and for your teen is no. If your teen doesn't want to marry someone who isn't on the same page spiritually, why would he choose to date the person? I'm not saying your teen has to consider marrying every person he dates, but any person he dates should be worthy of marriage. Therefore, the first question always is "Is she a Christian?"

Look at what the Bible says in 2 Corinthians 6:14–16: "You are not the same as those who do not believe. So do not join yourselves to them. Good and bad do not belong together. Light and darkness cannot share together. How can Christ and Belial, the devil, have any agreement? What can a believer have together with a nonbeliever? The temple of God cannot have any agreement with idols, and we are the temple of the living God" (NCV). When you choose to unite with a nonbeliever, it's as if you're setting up a pagan idol in God's temple. That's serious stuff. God warns us against making idols and worshipping other gods. In this case, opposites do not attract.

Dating a non-Christian may seem to be an innocent activity. A Christian teen might think dating can result in the conversion of a boyfriend or girlfriend. But the passage in 2 Corinthians warns that you're walking on dangerous ground when you choose to unite (even for just a few dates) with someone who rejects God. Dating a non-Christian is more likely to pull the Christian teen away from Christ than to draw the non-Christian teen toward God.

Explain to your teen that deciding not to date non-Christians does not mean she is judging them or refusing to spend time with them. Rather, it means she is striving to protect God's temple—her body. Jesus ate meals with prostitutes, liars, thieves, murderers, and the like, but He did so to point them to His Father. There is a huge distinction between accepting one who is lost and dating or marrying someone who is lost.

## Know Your Teen's Dating Patterns

As your teen starts dating, he will develop an individual perspective on dating. Ask yourself these questions:

- Does my teen care very little about dating, or is she desperate for a date?
- When my teen starts a relationship, does he strive to make sure the relationship works at all costs?
- Does my teen bounce from one relationship to the next, always looking for the quick thrill of dating a new person?
- Is my teen interested in waiting to date until she meets "the one"?
- Does my teen view dating as just a fun time of hanging out with friends?
- Does my teen quickly fall in and out of love (or what he believes is love)?

The answers to such questions will help you better understand how your teen views dating. Being aware of her dating habits can help you recognize when she might be developing unhealthy patterns. For instance, if your daughter believes that a boyfriend will make her feel more secure, then she may be willing to do whatever she believes is necessary to hold on to him. Or if your son views dating as a game of hooking up, then he is developing a harmful pattern of using girls.

The better connected you are to your teen, the better prepared you will be to help him maneuver through the dating process and deal with potential insecurities and struggles.

### Pray Before Each Date

In order to help your teen maintain dating relationships that honor God, I highly recommend that you pray together. In Luke 22:40 Jesus instructed His disciples, "Pray that you will not fall into temptation." That's what you should pray as well.

When I tell a roomful of teens to pray with their parents before dates, some of them give me a hard time, so you will need to take the lead on this. Prayer sets the tone for the date and helps your teen establish a God-centered foundation for any potential relationship.

### Help Set Physical Boundaries

Teens wonder how far is too far. They have heard youth pastors and other speakers talk about purity, heart, and intention. I believe the physical-boundary question deserves a simple, straightforward, and memorable answer. Teens should draw imaginary horizontal lines across their date's shoulders and knees and never touch anything between the lines. It's also important to spell out that holding hands or sharing a brief hug or a kiss on the cheek or lips may be appropriate but that prolonged hugging and kissing, french kissing, touching breasts, petting and fondling of clothed or unclothed genital areas, mutual masturbation, oral sex, any sort of nudity, anal intercourse, and genital intercourse are never acceptable before marriage.

Don't hesitate to be clear about what is and is not appropriate. The world talks about these things with your teen, but she needs to hear about them from you. You and your teen can apply every other step in this chapter to her dating life, but if you do not help her set clear, God-honoring physical boundaries, it will be only a matter of time before she gets tripped up.

## Help Develop an Exit Plan

I tell teens, "You cannot wait for a fire to erupt before you figure out how you will escape. Don't wait until you're already in a tempting or compromising situation to figure out how to avoid it." Before your teen's next date, he needs to do the following:

- Clarify what type of events and places are off-limits. For example, your teen should explain to his date, "We will never be alone in a tempting environment, such as a bedroom."
- Be prepared to say no.
- Be ready and willing to escape from a compromising situation or any situation that makes him uncomfortable.
- Be willing and ready to exit a relationship if it does not honor God.

Make it clear that your teen can and should call you at any time, day or night, and that you will pick her up wherever she is.

## Expect Respect

Respect is a big deal! As parents, we have to understand that our kids learn respect and disrespect by watching us and observing the world around them.

First, a few thoughts for parents of sons. Every boy should respect girls. As a parent of a son, it is your job to teach him to respect and honor women. You must nurture a respectful attitude and show your son what this looks like on a practical level.

Almost weekly, we hear about another incident of domestic violence or sexual assault. Use these moments to talk to your son about these important issues. You can't assume he already knows. Of course, the first step is to model respect. Demonstrate for your son how to value girls. Dads, if you are married, the way you treat your spouse will deeply affect your son. How do you speak to your wife, both at home and in public? Do you demonstrate respect for your wife's opinions and feelings? How do you treat her when no one is looking?

Moms, your influence is invaluable. You have the opportunity to give your son insight into the feminine mind and heart. Tell him what it means to be respected instead of diminished or ignored. How can he communicate respect in big and small ways to all the girls and women in his life? Your son will draw great security in watching you exemplify respect in your marriage.

Look for teachable moments to instill in your son the importance of treating girls respectfully. Talk about what love is and is not. Help establish healthy boundaries for his dating life: the kind of girl he should date, how he should treat a girl on a date, the amount of time the two of them should spend alone, parties and other settings to avoid, and so on. Encourage him to meet his date's parents and to look them in the eyes when speaking with them. Emphasize that relationships are about more than just him and his date. Explain that she has a family and that how he treats her also affects her family.

Be the parent your son needs you to be and hold him accountable. In particular, teen boys need to know there are things that are absolutely unacceptable. Sexist remarks or jokes often can be a red flag, signaling a deeper belief or pattern of devaluing women. If you hear your son making such a comment or joking about girls in a disrespectful way, speak up. If you stay silent, you're sending the message "What you just said is no big deal." Sometimes you may need to sit him down and say, "This is unacceptable." Tell him why and then challenge him to do better. Teen boys need to be taught the following:

- A girl is a valuable person with valid feelings.
- You should never pressure a girl into doing something she doesn't want to do.
- If a girl tells you no, that doesn't mean she needs to be convinced or that she's asking for more. No means no.
- Talk to girls in person, not just via text, and look into their eyes.

For parents of daughters, every girl should respect boys and expect respect from boys. Teen girls need to be taught the following:

- You should never compromise who you are to get the attention of a boy.
- Be able to clearly articulate your expectations and convictions before going on a date.
- Expecting respect begins with respecting yourself. This includes how you dress.
- Respect yourself enough to never use your body or your attire to attract the interest or affection of another person.

Have your son or daughter consider these questions:

- Do you ever feel mistreated by someone you are dating?
- Does he or she make you feel dumb after you've said something?
- Do you often say nothing because you're afraid of being corrected?
- Has a date ever abused you verbally or physically?
- Does he or she belittle or make fun of you for going to church, praying, or reading the Bible?

If your teen answers yes to any of these questions, he probably is not receiving the respect he deserves. If he tries to come up with excuses for why the person he is dating has been disrespectful, you both have a bigger problem. Too many teens believe they don't deserve to be treated well, but that's *never* true.

## Beginning Again

I have spoken with countless teens who feel guilty about their past sexual choices. These teens suffer guilt either from having gone all the way or from having gone further than they wanted to. If you've been there, then you know it's not easy to let go of sexual baggage. Satan has convinced many that because they've made mistakes, they can never start over and honor God in their future dating lives. But God's forgiveness is not conditional. When we ask for it, He forgives us. "If we confess our sins, he is faithful and just and will forgive us our sins and purify us from all unrighteousness" (1 John 1:9). God says, "I will forgive you. Period." If your teen has made mistakes, she needs to know that every day is a new day with God. The past is the past. The important thing is to avoid making the same wrong choices again. This is where you may be needed.

Your teen will need your help in developing a plan of action to avoid being in the same environment where he previously failed. This may mean walking away from a harmful dating relationship. Unless he takes drastic measures to avoid repeating certain mistakes, he might end up in a vicious cycle of constantly failing in the same areas. Encourage your teen when he is feeling guilty. It can make all the difference in where his dating life goes in the future.

Again, never forget that your teen wants you to be involved in her life. She may not always show it, but your interest in what she values and enjoys is important. As you strive to communicate with her about all things dating, you may at first encounter a negative response. But don't give up. Instead, continue to ask questions and start conversations. Take it slow at first if necessary. Allow trust to build as you demonstrate your interest in her dating life. It will be well worth it.

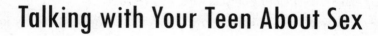

# 14

# Talking with Your Teen About Sex

I will never forget the day our younger daughter came home and said, "Guess what I learned in school, Daddy." I thought she might say something about current events or English vocabulary. She was in kindergarten, and I made a few wrong guesses. Finally, she exclaimed, "Today I learned how I was made!"

*What are they teaching kids in kindergarten these days?* I wondered. You probably can imagine the humor in the moment. My daughter's next question was "Daddy, do you know how I was made?"

"Yes, I know," I said.

To which she responded, "Well, tell me!" She wasn't ready to end the conversation.

"Why don't *you* tell *me* how you were made?" I asked.

Just as quickly, she responded with "No, Daddy. You tell me how you think I was made, and I'll let you know if you are right."

I've laughed often as I've remembered this story. It's the first conversation I can recall having with Brynnan about how she was made. It came earlier than I had expected. This conversation with my daughter reminded me of two things:

1. Our kids have questions about their sexuality.
2. As parents, we have to be willing to provide the answers.

The more I work with students, the more I realize that the topic of sex truly is about so much more than just the dos and don'ts. Body image, confidence, and self-worth all play a role in helping our sons and daughters make God-honoring choices with their sex lives.

Your words as a parent are powerful. Your input goes a long way toward helping your teen resist the world's lies. Satan works hard to confuse our kids. He tries to sell them lies that will convince them they are not strong, beautiful, wonderful, valuable, and worthy of love. Here are a few of his zingers:

- "Unless you have a perfect body, no one will ever love you or want to date you."
- "If you don't have a boyfriend or a girlfriend, you are a loser."
- "Having sex with your boyfriend or girlfriend is the only way to feel loved."
- "You'll never hold on to your boyfriend or girlfriend unless you have sex."
- "Everyone else is having sex, so if you want to fit in, you should too."

Parents ask how they can prevent their teens from having premarital sex. The sad truth is that you can do all the right things and your teen might still become sexually active. No matter how hard you pray and how clearly you communicate God's plan for sex, you can't control the choices your child makes. Ultimately, your teen will make his own decisions. Although you can't control his choices, you can make sure you have conversations about sex.

Caleb, a seventeen-year-old from Nashville, told me, "My parents have always been extremely open with me about dating and sex. I know exactly where they stand: they expect me to wait until marriage. It isn't always easy living up to their expectations. But knowing how they feel gives me the confidence to wait and do the right thing. I believe, with their support, this is something I can do!" Teens say they want their parents to have this talk with them. If you don't talk to your son or daughter, who will? Satan wants you to believe that this is someone else's responsibility, but he is lying. Your teen's body and mind are changing, and she is bombarded by messages saying that sex is no big deal.

How do you go about having this crucial conversation? What do you say? How do you become the number one source of sexual wisdom for your teen? It starts with keeping the lines of communication open.

## From "the Talk" to "the Talks"

You might think your son or daughter already has had enough of the sex talk. My response is "Enough is never enough." A dad told me, "I had the talk with my son when he was eleven. It was difficult to get through it, but I did it." You are playing with fire if you believe a onetime conversation is all it takes. We must be aggressive and unapologetic in communicating truths to our teens. It's no longer "the talk" but rather ongoing, consistent communication.

Teens not only want to talk to their parents about this but also *value* what their parents have to say. So where do you start? Here are ten broad themes that you need to communicate.

### 1. Invite Awkward Topics

Amy and I want our girls to trust us when it comes to any topic, no matter how awkward. My experience in counseling teens tells me that most are desperate for their parents' advice. While speaking at a student camp in Texas, I met Cedric, a sophomore. He said, "My dad hasn't really spoken much with me about anything, especially my dating life. He has never talked to me about girls or any of that stuff. I've just kind of figured it out on my own. I have made my share of mistakes with girls and doing things I know we shouldn't have. I know this isn't my dad's fault. I've made my own choices. I do wish he could have been more open with me about it all. Maybe things would have gone differently." Your kids need you to be willing to tolerate the discomfort of an awkward conversation.

## 2. Be Clear About What You Believe

My daughters attend a Christian school. They go to chapel twice a week at school and are required to take Bible courses every semester. Yet I've been shocked by the conversations my freshman daughter overhears at her school. She has been exposed to coarse language and stories about sex and masturbation from fellow students.

As a parent, you must consistently communicate God's guidelines for living a sexually blameless life. Before you do, perform a self-inventory. Do you believe there ever is a time when it is okay to have sex outside of marriage? What if a couple has dated for a long time or is engaged? You must solidify your answers in your mind and heart before talking to your teen.

Nowhere in Scripture does God give anyone the green light to have sex before marriage. We read in 1 Corinthians 6:18, "Flee from sexual immorality." The Greek word for sexual immorality is *porneia,* which refers to all sexual sin. God is saying, "Don't get close to it! It doesn't matter if you are in love, engaged, or going to prom. *Flee,* or run, from all sexual sin." Sharing this verse with your teen doesn't ensure that he won't face temptation. Still, it's a critical starting point. Remember, we live what we believe. The more you clearly articulate your beliefs about sex and emphasize that they are based in the truth of Scripture, the better equipped he will be.

Alycia, a seventeen-year-old, sent an email that confirms the importance of parents continuing to talk to their teens. Alycia wrote, "I really believe I will be a virgin on the day of my wedding. My parents have always talked to me about waiting. They challenged me to wait for that one special person. I'm not saying it's always easy, but I am committed, thanks to the input I received from my parents."

### 3. Rely on the Truth of Scripture

Satan wants your teen to fail in her pursuit of sexual purity. Scripture is your greatest resource to alert her to the danger. Keep looking for creative ways to get God's Word into her heart. In the context of conversations about sex, here are a couple of verses you might meditate on:

Flee from sexual immorality. All other sins a person commits are outside the body, but whoever sins sexually, sins against their own body. (1 Corinthians 6:18)

Marriage should be honored by everyone, and husband and wife should keep their marriage pure. God will judge as guilty those who take part in sexual sins. (Hebrews 13:4, NCV)

Consider having a family discussion that focuses on sexual purity. Hang out at the dinner table to talk about God's plan for His children's sex lives. Encourage each family member to find a verse or passage of Scripture that the family can memorize together. Then display the verses in a high-traffic area in your home. That way each of you will see them throughout the day. When a moment of sexual temptation comes your teen's way, and it will come, Scripture can be a critical weapon he uses to say no.

## 4. Highlight the Benefits of Purity

Teens are weary of hearing everyone say, "Don't have sex!" Why? Because most pro-abstinence messages highlight only the negative consequences of having premarital sex. The teens have a good point.

Many well-intentioned adults, abstinence educators, pastors, and parents focus primarily on the negative side of the issue in an attempt to convince teens to say no. Most people, especially teens, don't respond well to negative persuasion. Focusing on the positive aspects of waiting and the reward that follows is far more persuasive.

Heather, age fifteen, told me, "I know sex outside of marriage is wrong. I've heard that from Mom, Dad, church, teachers, and my pastor for years! But I wish someone would spin it positive. I don't think I've ever heard my parents or pastor tell me something really good about sex. If sex is such a great thing from God, why don't we hear about how great it is?"

Start sharing positive aspects of waiting until marriage. If you waited yourself, share the joy that virginity brought to your wedding night, such as no guilt, comparison to a previous relationship, emotional baggage, or concern about passing on a disease. When teens choose to protect the gift of sex, rewards follow. As you communicate this message, you can show your teen how following God's plan will greatly reduce relational pain, regret, and emotional scars. It also will prevent contracting certain diseases or becoming pregnant.

God's plan is not designed to keep us from having fun. It is meant to protect our future fun.

## 5. Put the Focus on Honoring God

I recently counseled a teen girl and guy who admitted struggling with physical stuff in their relationship. The girl said, "As long as we don't go all the way, everything's okay, right?"

Her question made me realize how desperate this generation is to know that purity is about so much more than just saying no to going all the way. I no longer pray just that my daughters will be virgins when they get married. I also pray for their purity, which is more important. The word *virgin* can become an escape word for teens, one that gives them a false sense of complying with the rules. There are a number of physical acts that two people can do on dates without going "all the way" in order to maintain their virginity. But all the physical activity that leads up to sex can be just as damaging spiritually, physically, and emotionally.

So instead of trying to scare her with horror stories, ask your teen, "How far is too far?" But *before* that, think about the question behind the stated question. Teens are asking, without using the words, "How much can I get away with?" This is a dangerous question. If they are intent on testing the boundaries while avoiding genital or anal intercourse, they will find they are on a path that leads to physical tragedy. Their bodies were not created to come right up to the line, sexually, and then suddenly stop. God warns us in 1 Corinthians 6:18 to avoid porneia—any sexual sin—at all cost. We can't even have a hint of it, as Ephesians 5:3 says, because God understands that sometimes all it takes is a little push to send us over the edge.

## 6. Provide Practical Answers

What is the answer to the question "How far is too far?" First, the key is sexual purity. Challenging your teen to pursue a lifestyle of purity will help him understand the stakes. This approach is more effective than trying to define how far is too far. He needs to know that God's plan for his sex life is freedom—freedom from emotional baggage, regret, comparisons, and consequences. God knows far better than we do that choosing to stray outside His plan correlates to one thing—pain. He created the plan: one man plus one woman for one lifetime. Your teen needs to clearly understand that anyone who chooses a plan other than this will eventually suffer. No matter how convincing the world can be, at some point and in some way, choosing the world's way over God's way will hurt him.

For some teens, a kiss leads to trouble. For others, it might be a long hug or a touch on the leg. This is why I believe that the answer is "Too far is anything more than a kiss. And sometimes you're not even ready for a kiss."

## 7. Remember, a Kiss Is Like a Doughnut

Nothing beats one (or five) hot, steamy Krispy Kreme doughnuts. Some people might believe that the pleasure of these sweet delights is limited to the sensation of sucrose hitting one's tongue. Not so. The fact is that you continue to taste sugar as it works its way through your body.

Special taste buds designed to detect sweet-tasting stuff exist all over your tongue. When something sweet hits these cells, a Yum! signal is sent straight to the brain. As you digest sugar, enzymes break it down into glucose and fructose. In the small intestine additional taste cells register Yum! Out of the small intestine, transporter proteins carry the molecules through the bloodstream to the pancreas. And guess what? In the pancreas, the same reaction: Yum!

The sugar sensation we experience is a full-body one. And, you guessed it, the same is true when it comes to a kiss, especially for an impressionable teen. The world wants our sons and daughters to believe that a kiss is as simple as choosing an original or chocolate-glazed Krispy Kreme. But it's not. A kiss is an intimate experience, and God wants us to experience the "Oh my word!" all-over reaction when it comes to a kiss. Your teen needs to hear, often, that a kiss should be reserved for an incredibly special relationship. Not every person who wants to date your son or daughter gets the privilege of a good-night kiss.

## 8. Reinforce the Purpose of Dating

Ask your teen, "What kind of person do you hope to marry one day?" At first, she might try to laugh it off. If that happens, ask again. I'm confident she already has an answer, even if she hasn't given it much thought.

When Bailey was nine, she accompanied me to a conference. While there, I asked the audience to write down their most important qualities for a future spouse. Bailey made her own list. I was thrilled when she included the following: treats me like I want to be treated, likes my daddy, is a Christian, and "If he can't take no, then the boy has got to go!"

Teens' lists may change as they mature. The important thing is that they begin to think about the qualities they want in a spouse. When your teen begins to date, his list can help gauge whether a person is datable. As we've already discussed, dating is preparation for marriage, and your teen should not be dating (seriously or not) anyone he wouldn't consider marrying. The important challenge from you to him should be "Never compromise your list."

## 9. Teach Your Teen That No Is a Good Word

I love hearing that my daughters have no problem standing up for what they know is right. I remind them often of the power of the word *no*. I want my daughters to know that standing up for what they believe is worth it. Ephesians 5:15 instructs, "Be very careful, then, how you live— not as unwise but as wise." We need to show our kids the power of standing up for right and saying no to wrong.

"How can I say no without hurting someone's feelings?" I get this question a lot. Many teens want to say no to a date's physical advances, but they are afraid of hurting the date's feelings. Here's what I tell my daughters. If a guy wants you to do stuff you don't want to do—and, more importantly, God doesn't want you to do—you shouldn't care if you hurt his feelings. If he gets angry, he's not worth worrying about. I remind them, "*No* is a good word—use it."

We read in 2 Timothy 1:7, "God has not given us a spirit of fear and timidity, but of power, love, and self-discipline" (NLT). Teaching our kids to be confident in what they believe to be true and right will serve them well for a lifetime.

## 10. Emphasize That It's All About God

There are many reasons for your teen to maintain sexual purity until marriage. The reasons include avoiding guilt, never facing fear over contracting a sexually transmitted disease, and not having to worry about an unwanted pregnancy. Each of these is an extremely important reason. However, the number one reason to say no to sex, and all things sex related, is because God said so.

As our creator and heavenly Father, God doesn't need another reason for why we should obey what He says. God said it, so that's the end of it. But the cool thing is that God does have another reason: if teenagers choose purity before marriage, they will find freedom. Whether they realize it or not, that's what they really want. Freedom is what we all want.

People will rationalize premarital sex by saying, "This is your life, so you should live the way you want." This statement is ultimately about freedom—freedom to live the way you want, freedom to find the best in life, freedom to have what will make you happiest. The world says, "Go ahead. Indulge. You deserve it. Everyone is doing it. No strings attached. This is true freedom."

Ironically, we can find true freedom only in Christ (see Galatians 5:1). Many teens believe that if they choose God's way, they will have to give up the freedom to live the way they want, especially when it comes to sex. The world's version of sexual freedom may make them feel great at first, but they will find that it makes them feel more imprisoned because they're weighed down by fear of getting caught or they may face some really un-fun consequences. Worst of all, pursuing the world's sexual freedom takes them further away from the real freedom found in Christ. This freedom is built on Him—the best, the strongest, the eternal foundation—and it never will leave them feeling trapped and empty. God's plan for sexual purity isn't about giving up freedom. God's plan is about being free.

## God's Plans for a Good Future

Before my daughter turned two, we bought her a baby pool. She loved it. One time she was swimming and I needed to go into the office for a phone call, so I took her out of the pool. She threw a fit, something we always said our children would never do. She was upset because just moments before, she was swimming and having a great time. Now she was being forced to go inside. In her young mind, she thought I was trying to keep her from having fun. But as you know, I was trying to protect her. I would never leave her alone in a pool filled with water. There could have been a huge tragedy waiting.

The same is true with God. He does not do things to keep your teen from having fun. Rather, His plans are designed to protect your child's future fun within marriage. When it comes to sex, or any choice your teen faces that might lead her outside God's will, He knows there will be tragedy waiting if the choice is made to "swim alone." Fortunately, your teen has you on her side.

It is important to note that embracing a life of purity also applies to nonsexual challenges and choices, such as being honest, taking responsibility for one's words and actions, being generous, standing up for what is right, maintaining personal integrity, never cheating, and taking a stand for those who are bullied or are victims of injustice. Making an impure choice in situations like these can destroy a teenager's confidence, self-image, reliability, and reputation.

Impure behaviors and habits beyond sex can destroy a person's character. Don't be afraid to discuss these sensitive issues so your teen will be equipped to navigate our world of temptations and lies. Remember, you are the parent. Be the parent your teen needs you to be.

# 15

# Helping Your Teen
# Find Wise Friends

When I was ten years old, my dad took a new job. My parents told me it was going to be a good move for my dad's career. The job came with great perks for my dad and our family, including a salary increase and a new car. It also meant we could build a new home. In spite of the blessings, all I remember thinking was that we'd have to move. It was hard leaving my childhood home. I knew I'd be starting over with no friends. At the time, I didn't know that the move to a new city would be the beginning of a friendship that would remain strong for many years.

Louis was in my grade, and it felt as though we became best friends almost immediately. We loved sports, music, cars, and mischief. One time we rode our bikes over a cliff into the Buffalo River on a dare. Countless times we snuck out at night to go swimming in our neighborhood pool. We thought we were so clever waiting until my parents went to sleep. But one night we returned home to find the back door locked. We slept on the back porch that night, in our swimsuits.

One night we rode our bikes past a house with a lawn sprinkler operating in the front yard. We thought it would be a bright idea to turn the sprinkler toward the front door of the house and then ring the doorbell. I remember the guy opening the door just as the sprinkler soaked him with water. I also remember the call later that night. The homeowner attended our church and knew my parents. Dad made sure I never forgot that night.

Louis and I didn't always make the smartest decisions, but we did hold each other accountable when it came to the stuff that mattered most. It may have been part internal instinct and part godly protection. Either way, other than a few silly (and borderline stupid) choices, Louis and I graduated without making any major mistakes.

Close friendships matter at all ages, but especially in the teen years. One comment from a friend can change how teens feel about a situation or themselves. This probably is true for your teen as well.

I asked my older daughter why her friends matter to her. She said, "My best friend is someone I trust completely. I can't imagine life without her." It concerns me that my daughter expressed such strong sentiments about someone who isn't part of her family and could turn on her in a moment.

I know that having the right friends matters to my daughter. I also know that her definition and my definition of "right friends" may not always align. Bailey has some friends who have made unkind comments to her. She is a very loyal friend and has this beautiful way of forgetting and forgiving. As her daddy, I can learn from such grace. I also know that I have to help protect her from those who might use her loyalty and grace against her.

Your teen's friends matter because the friends are a crucial link in building him up or tearing him down. Your teen spends hours each week with friends. Friends are people who greatly influence how he talks, thinks, acts, dresses, and approaches life. It is critical he understands this.

If your child is a preteen, her current BFF can change as quickly as the weather. Teens are more likely to have a core group of friends who have become an integral part of their lives. Either way, your child needs your input, advice, prayer, and guidance as she chooses friends.

## Friend or Fool

Scripture is full of wisdom about friendships. Proverbs 13:20 encapsulates everything God wants us to know about choosing healthy friendships: "Walk with the wise and become wise, for a companion of fools suffers harm." I hope you will read this verse as a family. Make sure to point out both the promise and the warning from God as it relates to friendship.

The promise is simple: the one who "walk[s] with the wise . . . become[s] wise." A wise person knows the difference between right and wrong and consistently chooses to do what's right. Teens who spend time with wise friends—friends who know right from wrong and consistently choose right—will grow in wisdom. Wise friends offer good advice in times of need because they believe that God's ways are right. Simply put, wise friends will help make your teen a better person. Each member of your family should ask himself or herself, "Do my friends make me a better person?"

The warning in Proverbs 13:20 is just as clear. If you hang out with fools, you'll become a fool. Even worse, "a companion of fools suffers harm." If your teen spends time with fools, or with those who consistently choose wrong, bad things will happen. This verse doesn't say bad stuff *might* happen. God's Word is clear. A companion of fools *will* suffer harm. If your teen chooses to hang out with fools, he will get hurt. Each member of your family should answer this question: "Have I done things with my friends that have hurt me or gotten me in trouble?"

This Scripture verse doesn't list a bunch of activities that lead to harm, such as drinking and driving or cheating on a test. Even though such choices could lead to serious consequences, this verse doesn't focus on actions. Rather, it focuses on *who* your teen is with. It is as if God is saying, "If you spend time with a fool, you will suffer." This is why she needs your input in choosing friends who are wise by God's standards.

These six suggestions will help you discuss with your teen how to choose friends wisely. An open conversation can help steer him away from being "a companion of fools."

### 1. Encourage Honesty

Encourage your teen to honestly consider how friends affect the way she lives, dresses, thinks, and acts. A wise friend will never ask your teen to do something that conflicts with the Bible. She must consistently evaluate friendships by asking the tough questions.

In a friendship (or dating relationship), one person typically has more control in the relationship. One of the toughest things to ask is "Who is in control?" More times than not, teens make wrong choices because they become followers and allow unwise friends to lead the way. If your teen is a natural leader and makes good choices, others will follow his positive example. It's important that he learns to control situations rather than make choices based on what other people say is right.

Here are some questions to ask your teen to consider and to talk through with her:

- Do I have a friend who consistently pressures me to do something I know is against God's will?
- Do my friends make fun of me when I pray, read the Bible, or go to church?
- Do I have a friend who often lies to family members about his or her whereabouts?

- Do my friends push me to watch movies, listen to music, or view websites that my parents think are inappropriate?
- Do my friends encourage me to lie to my parents or disobey their wishes?

Proverbs 18:2 says, "Fools find no pleasure in understanding but delight in airing their own opinions." If your teen gets suggestions, support, and advice from friends who don't know God, such input will shape his belief system and, ultimately, lifestyle. If God said it, He means it. If it's in the Bible, it's truth. If you and your teen take God at His word, the reality is that any friends who have not chosen lives that please God are fools. If your child continues to spend time with such friends, he will suffer consequences.

God wants us to have fun with good friends. But He also knows what can happen if we choose the wrong friends, which is why He has given us such a serious warning. Your goal is to help your teen honestly evaluate the influence her friends wield and then move forward with friendships that honor God.

## 2. Teach Discretion

Communicate the importance of using discretion when it comes to choosing friends and making choices involving friends. Discretion is the freedom to choose. When your teen loses control over a situation, he loses freedom to make wise choices. Proverbs 2:11 reads, "Discretion will protect you, and understanding will guard you." Poor choices almost always lead to pain. Urge him to ask, *Do my friends push me closer to God, or do they pull me away from Him?*

Answering this question honestly can be one of the easiest ways for teens to distinguish between healthy, God-honoring relationships and ones that do not honor God. Look what Kendra wrote about her high school experience: "I chose to be someone other than me because I was so concerned about pleasing a few friends. Ultimately, I have no one to blame but myself. I chose them as friends, and now I have to live with the results of my choices."

## 3. Establish Healthy Boundaries

If your teen has a friend who isn't a good influence, it can be tricky to make her end that friendship or even put boundaries on it. If you intervene, it can cause friction. The place to start is with your child. Does she have the strength to make the right choices without your intervention? If so, good. If she does end the friendship, she may go through a season of solitude. This will be difficult, and your sensitivity as a parent is important.

If your teen does not want to end a harmful friendship, it may be necessary for you to step in. Consider writing down the qualities and parameters you and your teen agree will contribute to healthy relationships with wise friends. He will need specific guidelines for interacting with friends who don't fit the parameters. This might begin with defining when, where, and for how long he can interact with this person or group. Of course, there are extreme situations when you have to tell your child to end the friendship.

My friend Taylor told me about his daughter, Amber, who is now out of college and living in California. Taylor and his wife had to step in when Amber was a high school junior because she needed to establish serious relationship boundaries. She had chosen several unhealthy friendships and didn't have the strength to break free. Taylor established rules that his daughter had a hard time following, and ultimately he and his wife prevented Amber from seeing one former friend.

He said, "It's been six years since we went through it all. Now things are so good between us. Her mother and I had to make some tough decisions then, but I know we did what was right and best for Amber." Amber recently visited her parents. She talked a lot about the difficult years in high school. She said, "Dad, I know I didn't make it easy on you and Mom back then, but I want you to know how thankful I am that you loved me enough to make those tough choices for me. I didn't like it at the time, but I now know absolutely that you were doing what was best and safest for me!"

What might it look like for you to establish stronger boundaries—even physical boundaries—to help your teen avoid contact with a harmful friend or group of friends? You may need to have her change schools, sports teams, school buses, and so on. You may need to more closely monitor cell phone and social media use or even take away her cell phone privileges for a while. Obviously, these are not easy things to implement. But parenting isn't always fun or easy, is it?

## 4. Go Beyond Acceptance

Most teens gravitate toward friends who accept them. We all do this to some extent. But what happens when the wrong group of friends accepts your teen? Or when acceptance becomes his only criterion for friendships? I tell my daughters to be choosy about their friends. Your child should not look down on others or avoid associating with teens who are not Christians. But it is imperative for teens to be wise in choosing their friends. And it is possible for other Christian teens to be a negative influence.

An important thing to consider is *intention.* Jesus hung out with people from all walks of life, but He didn't hang out with people just to have a good time. He always tried to point His friends—and enemies—to His Father. Is your teen surrounding herself with friends who spur one another on in their faith (see Hebrews 10:24)? Or is she intentionally spending time with someone who is not a believer? If so, make sure she is ready for such a challenge. Even with the best of intentions, not every teen possesses the spiritual maturity to undertake such a responsibility.

## 5. Invite Accountability

I have a close friend who asks me tough questions about my private life. He helps ensure that I keep working to overcome my struggles, temptations, and trip-ups. Sometimes his to-the-point questions seem a little threatening. Because I know he'll be asking, I make sure I am striving for growth in these areas. Such accountability helps.

Jesus demonstrated accountability when He assembled a group of twelve followers and lived life with them. As your teen matures, he needs friends who are willing to hold one another accountable. Go out of your way to encourage friendships with other kids who will serve as age-appropriate accountability partners for your teen. Stock the fridge, order a pizza (or ten), and give him and his friends the green light each week to hang out in your living room. (I can't think of many greater returns on your investment.)

Encouraging your teen to maintain accountability with others will help her on many levels. First, it will let her know that she is not alone in the battle against the Enemy. Second, it will invigorate her to know that others are praying for her. Additionally, it will help her celebrate moments of victory on her spiritual journey.

I know a group of teens who meet every Sunday night at Starbucks to talk about life, encourage one another, read Scripture, pray, and celebrate one another's spiritual victories.

## 6. Know Your Teen's Friends

I can't stress enough how important it is for you to get to know the friends of your teen. Keep learning about the individuals in his inner circle by checking to see who he is following on social media, identifying his best friend, and keeping track of his friends who are around the most.

Getting to know your teen's friends isn't always as simple as asking who she spends time with. Even if she tells you names, you will need to dig more deeply to identify the beliefs, habits, and spiritual maturity of the people she considers friends.

Amy and I built a fire pit in the backyard and purchased a pool table for the basement. Because our daughters both play sports, we also purchased a volleyball net and installed a basketball court in the backyard. We hope our girls' friends and teammates will want to hang out at our house. This gives us the opportunity to get to know their friends while also allowing us the privilege of positively influencing all these teens.

Your desire to stay connected with your teen and his friends may involve spending money. Think for a moment about what is important to him (and his friends), and then use that knowledge. If they are into movies, a Netflix subscription may be the winning ticket to get them to spend time at your house. If it's singing and music, gaming consoles such as PlayStation, Wii, and Xbox have dance and sing-along games such as *SingStar: Ultimate Party* and *Sing It*. You never need a good excuse to have a karaoke night. Whether you need to buy an Apple TV or simply throw a pizza party after the game on Friday night, invest what it takes to become better acquainted with your teen's friends.

I also advise you to build relationships with the parents of your teen's friends. If your child is not in your home, she is most likely in the home of another set of parents. Not only do her friends influence her, but her friends' parents do as well.

Several times a year Amy and I host a party and invite our daughters' friends, along with their parents and siblings. It has been wonderful to get to know other parents. This has provided an excellent opportunity to express our concerns and values.

What works for our family may not necessarily work for yours. The important thing to remember is that our kids need our help when it comes to the friends they choose. Use wisdom, pray a lot, and be creative as you help your teen navigate this critically important area of life.

# 16

# The Top Ten Questions Teens Are Asking

If you're like me, you hit the ground running as soon as the alarm goes off. I love the turn my life has taken and the fact that my daily schedule often is determined by what my daughters are doing. And in my work, as I listen to teens ask questions and tell their stories, I also think of my daughters. Will Bailey and Brynnan face these issues as well? Will they struggle to figure out who they are? Will they make poor choices that cause them stress and pain? Do you ever wonder how your teen's friends, professors, employers, and culture will influence him? Paul issued this warning in Colossians 2:8: "See to it that no one takes you captive by philosophy and empty deceit, according to human tradition, according to the elemental spirits of the world, and not according to Christ" (ESV). A multitude of voices works to attract the attention of your teen, filling him with ideas and input that are beyond your control.

## Be Prepared

What is your teen talking about? More importantly, what is your teen thinking about? She is asking or will be asking a number of questions. It is critical that you be prepared with answers. Based on my years spent counseling and speaking to teens, here are the ten most common questions teens ask.

### 1. Is it okay that I long to feel secure and accepted?

A teen named Jamie wrote to me, saying, "I am a Christian and I do love Jesus and want to live for Him. But I have felt guilty for two years because I have been having sex with my boyfriend since I was fourteen. I know it is wrong. I know that God's Word is clear on all of this. But my boyfriend said he would break up with me if I said no. He told me that this is what a girl should be willing to do with her boyfriend, if she really loves him." Sadly, Jamie's story is not uncommon.

Jason, a high school senior, told me that he sent nude pictures of himself to his girlfriend. He said, "My dad's a high school principal at a Christian school. I've always been raised to know right from wrong, and I know how much my parents love me. But there are times, even when I know what I should and should not do, that I still choose to do things that I hope will make me feel more loved by my girlfriend." Another teen boy I know as a Christ follower explained it like this: "Just because I know what is right doesn't mean that I always choose right. There are times when I do things with my friends that I absolutely know I shouldn't. I can look back and clearly see that my choices were selfishly made in an attempt to get and keep the attention of people I want to be accepted by."

Students I counsel, many of whom are Christians, often confide their strong desire to feel secure and accepted by their peers. The desire to be accepted often is more important to them than their desire to honor God. I believe these teens have failed to grasp that they were created to find their meaning, purpose, and significance in God.

Our challenge as parents is to help our kids understand that they were created by a loving Father who wants nothing more than for them to have intimate relationships with Him. As you help your teen spend time with God, read the Bible, and pray, the confidence that comes from a greater sense of belonging to God can and will help him learn to look to God first for significance. This will help him turn away from the world as his source of security and acceptance. Of course, the process takes time. The critical step for you is to continue creating moments to discuss the normal need your teen has to feel secure and to share the amazing truth that such a need will be fulfilled as he grows in his relationship with God.

## 2. What if I'm not perfect enough?

Countless messages in our culture spread the lie that our kids just aren't *enough*. Many teen girls believe that unless they look and dress like Victoria's Secret models, they are of little value. Meanwhile, teen boys are also encouraged to get the right body, drive the right car, and learn to party like a rock star in order to have a perfect life. Everywhere they turn, there is a song, movie, commercial, magazine ad, billboard, or other prominent message telling teens that their money, prestige, body, and social status define them. Your role is to defuse and deconstruct these messages.

Psalm 139:14 declares, "I praise you because I am fearfully and wonderfully made; your works are wonderful, I know that full well." Knowing that God carefully created your teen doesn't change the fact that she may have pimples or not like her nose. Just because you convey the truth of Psalm 139 doesn't mean that tomorrow your child will look in the mirror and love what's there. But such a reality also doesn't minimize the truth that God created her exactly as He wants her to be.

For teens to see themselves through God's eyes, they have to overcome the world's indoctrination that they see their perceived flaws and nothing else. Their ability to see themselves as God intended requires learning to look beyond the things they don't like, as well as the things they don't have. It calls for realizing they have been created exactly the way God wanted.

God has an amazing plan for your teen, but Satan works hard to convince him that the reflection in the mirror will never be enough. You must work just as hard to help him see otherwise.

### 3. Will Mom and Dad make it?

Your teen wants you and your spouse to remain committed to each other. If you are married, she longs to see that your marriage is thriving. I have counseled a number of teens who tell me this is true. Our kids want our marriages to succeed just as much as we do. Almost every time I talk with students, the conversation turns to their parents' marriages. When things are tense at home, kids know it. Satan doesn't want your marriage to make it. This is why he works hard to convince you that prayer with your spouse, date nights, and continued communication with and focus on each other aren't important. However, you know otherwise. Taking steps every day to say "I love you" in big and small ways can have a profound impact on your marriage. Witnessing this intentionality can give your teen confidence that your marriage will last for the long haul.

If you are divorced, your child needs to be reminded that you and your ex still love him. Continue to remind him that the divorce wasn't his fault. Work hard not to fight in front of him. Find common ground in how you and your ex raise your child in separate homes. When you are with your teen, seize the moment. Strive to not be distracted by mobile devices, a ball game, or issues at work. Even though things didn't work out in your marriage, do your best to make sure he feels confident that he is the most important person in your life.

## 4. If God loves me, why does He allow bad things to happen?

Jared, a high school junior, wrote me to say, "My dad is gone, my mom is depressed, school sucks, and I'm sick of it. I try to do what is right, but nothing seems to go my way!"

I receive emails such as this one almost weekly. Often this important question arises when teens doubt God's love. I usually explain that God has given us the gift of free will. We are free to live how we choose, but often we make poor decisions. Why did God give us this freedom if He knew we could abuse it? He knew that in order for our love for Him to be genuine, it had to be something we choose.

We can decide to love and follow God, or we can go our own way. We have the freedom to choose whether to allow our desires to tempt us to sin. These realities in combination with Satan's influence in the world result in suffering, pain, and tragedy that God allows. We won't fully understand why God chooses not to intervene in every instance until we reach heaven. The Bible teaches, "Who knows a person's thoughts except their own spirit within them? In the same way no one knows the thoughts of God except the Spirit of God" (1 Corinthians 2:11). "As you do not know the path of the wind, or how the body is formed in a mother's womb, so you cannot understand the work of God, the Maker of all things" (Ecclesiastes 11:5).

When something bad happens to you, your teen, or someone you know, make sure you process it together, allowing space for grief or questioning. Meditate on the truth of Scripture: "The LORD is close to the brokenhearted and saves those who are crushed in spirit" (Psalm 34:18). Times of trial and suffering test our faith, and we often learn what it means to lean on God as we choose to trust Him. Trust means we give matters to God even when we don't understand or like the outcome. When you can't find a good reason for why such things happen, remember that God fully understands your pain. He suffered the greatest injustice of all by allowing His perfect Son, Jesus, to be arrested, beaten, spit on, cursed at, and then nailed to a cross to die. Jesus didn't deserve such treatment, but He sacrificed Himself for you and for all of us. Even when life is hard, God says, "I will not leave you nor forsake you" (Joshua 1:5, NKJV).

### 5. Are LGBTQ lifestyles wrong?

This is a tough question, and your teen needs you to answer it using biblical truth. You can point to Paul's words in the book of Romans: "Because people did those things, God left them and let them do the shameful things they wanted to do. Women stopped having natural sex and started having sex with other women. In the same way, men stopped having natural sex and began wanting each other. Men did shameful things with other men, and in their bodies they received the punishment for those wrongs" (1:26–27, NCV).

Because homosexuality and all lifestyles represented by the LGBTQ label have become more accepted in our society, saying they are wrong can make you and your teen seem intolerant. If people think you're intolerant, they're less likely to listen to what you have to say. But you also can't ignore what God's Word says. You'll meet people who believe that same-sex attraction is something people are born with or that gender identity is fluid. Your teen needs to know that God "created mankind in his own image, in the image of God he created them; male and female he created them" (Genesis 1:27). Anything outside the parameters God established is sin; it's not part of God's plan. Saying that to someone in person, however, is not as easy as writing it in this book.

It's critical for your teen to remember that she is not anyone's judge. Only God can serve in that role. This will help her be humble when sharing parts of God's Word that aren't easy for the other person to hear. We have to teach our children to stand for what is right, to hold firmly to what the Bible teaches, and to know that there will be times when we will be at odds with the world.

When your teen encounters divisive issues such as this, he should communicate God's love while clarifying what the Bible says. It may seem impossible to do both, but God can do the impossible. Remember, sin is sin no matter if it's cheating on a test, running a red light, or giving in to same-sex attraction.

If your teen struggles personally with same-sex attraction or gender dysphoria, make it clear that she can always talk to you. Then guide her as she talks to God. Let her know that God loves her completely. Your teen's struggle is no surprise to Him, and He wants to help her break free of it. This will be almost impossible without your help. I also suggest that you seek out a Christian counselor who is experienced in helping people who struggle with similar issues. God is big enough to handle it and help anyone through it.

## 6. How do I know God's purpose for my life?

Some people have a clear sense at a young age of God's purpose for them, while others discover slowly over the course of many years what God has uniquely gifted them to do. If your teen doesn't yet have a clear vision of what to do with his life, it can be easy for him to doubt God. Helping your child understand the journey to discovering God's purpose for his life begins here: "Your eyes saw my unformed body; all the days ordained for me were written in your book before one of them came to be" (Psalm 139:16). We also know from Scripture that "the LORD will fulfill his purpose for me" (138:8, ESV).

God has a purpose for your teen and wants to help her fulfill it. While teenagers wait for clarity on their big-picture life purpose, their daily purpose is to point other people to God. Your teen's greatest purpose is to be a mirror that reflects Him to the world. We might wish God would give us each a road map and daily schedule detailing what we should do, where we should go, to whom we should speak, and what we should avoid. That way we would never second-guess our choices or wonder, *What if?* And we'd always be certain to follow His purpose for our lives. However, knowing the answer to every question about the future soon would become boring. There would be no wonder, adventure, or anticipation. We would never have to figure anything out for ourselves or seek God's guidance. Life would be routine, robotic, and meaningless.

Thankfully, God didn't create us to be robots. Instead, He wants us to learn what it means to trust Him, believing He has it all figured out. Finding our purpose isn't about discovering all the answers today. Instead, it's about discovering what it means to trust God every step of the way.

### 7. If I'm good, will I go to heaven?

Shannon is a freshman who lives in California. I first met her when I was speaking at a camp she attended. Upon returning home she wrote, "My best friend is a really good person. She isn't a Christian, but she lives better than most Christians I know. Do you think she will get to go to heaven one day? She loves everyone so much and is the nicest person I know." Shannon is allowing her emotions and her love for her friend to dictate her beliefs. Satan has convinced many teens that access to heaven is determined by what a person does rather than what a person believes. According to Satan's lie, God wouldn't send a nice person to hell.

We have to help our children see past the emotion to the truth of Scripture. Ephesians 2:8–9 reads, "You have been saved by grace through believing. You did not save yourselves; it was a gift from God. It was not the result of your own efforts, so you cannot brag about it" (NCV). Jesus Himself said, "I am the way and the truth and the life. No one comes to the Father except through me" (John 14:6). Jesus Christ came to earth, lived a sinless life, died on a cross for every sin ever committed, conquered sin and death, came back to life, and now offers a personal relationship with Him and access to heaven for anyone who chooses to receive Him as savior. It is your responsibility to reinforce this truth in your teen's mind and heart and to help him share the good news with friends.

## 8. How should I deal with my secret struggles?

I know many teens who harbor secrets about their bodies, their pasts, their families, and their choices. I bet your teen has secrets too. Of course, not all secrets are sin. I meet people all the time who share their secrets with me, which leads to freedom. Proverbs 28:13 tells us, "Whoever conceals their sins does not prosper, but the one who confesses and renounces them finds mercy." Secrets can be powerful, weighing a person down in regret, worry, doubt, and fear.

We know that sin thrives in darkness. Whenever we expose secrets, however, we take away the power they exert over our families. We have to keep the lines of communication open with our teens. It is important to help them understand that God can bring light to the darkness in a way that is freeing. The tiniest bit of faith can transform a desperate situation into an opportunity for His amazing grace to come in, cleanse, and restore. God can make right the things in your teen's past that seem impossible to repair.

Satan wants your teen to believe that her secrets are something to feel ashamed of. He wants her to believe she should never talk to anyone about them, particularly Mom and Dad. He wants to convince your child that no one will understand. Help her reject such lies. If your teen has secrets, she is not weird, dysfunctional, or a freak. She is normal! We all have secrets. The difference between people who overcome their problems and those who stay trapped by them is belief that God's truth is stronger than Satan's lies.

The key is to start a conversation with your teen, to keep asking questions, and to help him see the answers in God's Word. God knows what's happening in his heart and life. The Bible proclaims, "Praise be to the Lord, to God our Savior, who daily bears our burdens" (Psalm 68:19). And, "Come to me, all you who are weary and burdened, and I will give you rest" (Matthew 11:28).

If you suspect your teen's secrets are harming her, start with the truth that God knows all secrets. "Would not God have discovered it, since he knows the secrets of the heart?" (Psalm 44:21). God sees your teen as she is, and He loves her. God wants her to become all that He intends. Your teen might tell you the truth if you ask, but one secret typically leads to another, and she may not give you a straight answer. Almost weekly I hear from at least one Gen Z student (both boys and girls, but especially boys) who struggle with masturbation. When these teens share their secret struggle, they often reveal another secret: an addiction to pornography. I always tell them that the first step to hope and healing is admitting that something needs to change.

Let your teen know that admitting to a problem can be difficult. But once people open up, they often feel a great sense of relief. If you suspect a problem but your teen is unwilling to talk about it, suggest that he approach someone else, such as a school counselor, coach, youth pastor, doctor, or nurse. Or suggest he write you a note if the topic feels too difficult to bring up in conversation. One father told me that his son did exactly this: he wrote him a letter about his secret struggle with porn. The father wrote back and told his son that during college, he struggled with the same secret. The two met and discussed their secrets and have grown immensely as dad and son.

Help your teen identify the trouble that triggers the secrets. Harmful outward behavior typically is one way people react to inner emotional tension or pain. What feelings or situations cause secret behavior? It could be anger, pressure to be perfect, relationship trouble, or a painful loss or trauma, or it might stem from being criticized or mistreated. Many teens have trouble figuring this out on their own.

It can be easier to observe pain from a distance than to roll up our sleeves and help. But as parents committed to the best for our teens, we need to be proactive in helping them. It takes a while for most teens to sort through strong feelings and learn better ways of coping with stress. When talking begins, secrets lose their power and healing can start. If you feel as though you need help from a pastor or counselor, get it. Remember, there is hope. God can make all things beautiful in His time.

## 9. Can I mask my emotional pain with physical pain?

Teens dealing with internal pain often have a slogan: "Mask the pain with pain!" Eating disorders, the choking game, and cutting are coping mechanisms for many teens who struggle with deep emotional or psychological pain. One teen boy showed me his cutting scars, which started at his ankle, covered most of his leg, and continued up to his elbow. He told me, "Cutting is my escape. The hurt, the blood, and the whole thing just help me feel better." I asked, "The first time you cut, did it work? Did it stop the pain?" He said, "Not really."

Satan wants everyone to believe that their hurts should make them feel ashamed. He *doesn't* want my kids or yours to talk to anyone about the pain. He *does* want our kids to believe that self-inflicted pain will cover the real pain. We have to help our kids find relief from internal pain. This begins with talking, but it may also involve extensive therapy. If you believe that your teen is cutting or inflicting pain on herself, there are likely much deeper issues. Such issues can be addressed only by a qualified professional. I hope you never lose sight of the powerful role you play in facilitating conversation with your teen. Helping our kids find hope in every area of life begins with teaching them to talk about rather than be silent about their fears, doubts, and struggles.

## 10. Do my past and present define my future?

Teens are affected by life's challenges in ways that can break their spirits. A comment from a friend, a bad hair day, not making the starting lineup in basketball, or even just looking in the mirror can introduce disappointments, disruptions, and distractions that shape how they see life and themselves. This coupled with the regret of past choices can often mislead our teens into believing that their pasts limit and define their futures.

Particularly with regret, our kids need to know that the past is the past. Every day is a new day that invites them to begin again. The challenges our teens face often are beyond our control and theirs. But we can work to rebuild, repair, and replenish their hopes by helping them focus on the future and the beautiful things in their lives.

For boys, this means helping them see that who they are isn't defined by how recklessly they drive, how fast they run the forty, or how quickly their tweets get retweeted. Instead, their value comes from the truth that God has created them for greatness. Achieving true greatness is a lifelong journey of fully pursuing a life of obedience.

For girls, this means reminding them that regardless of their weight, whether they have a date to prom, and the amount of likes their social media posts attract, working to make God first in all areas of life will be a choice that comes with no regrets and a lifetime of fulfillment.

## Remain All In

Answering your teen's questions is an ongoing process. Today everything may seem great with your child. But Satan is patient. He waits for the right moment to slither into his life. Today it may be all good. The hope is that tomorrow also will be all good. That's why you need to continue to be all in!

Our kids want answers to tough questions, so we need to position ourselves as their go-to sources of truth and information. The more we tackle tough issues with them, the more they view us as trustworthy. So keep working to have the answers. Be strategic in asking the right questions. And when you don't have the answers, let your teen know that you will work to get the answers she needs.

# 17

# Helping Your Teen Identify His or Her Purpose

A person's true purpose in life is about much more than winning earthly acclaim or amassing financial wealth. Jesus understood this. From the virgin birth to the empty tomb and ultimately to His return to heaven, Jesus had one purpose: to make God known to every person He encountered. Every day Jesus's life exemplified this purpose. His final charge to all Christ followers defined the purpose to which we, too, are called: "Go and make disciples of all nations" (Matthew 28:19). This also is the primary call on your teen's life: to share the good news of the Savior who gave His life for everyone.

## Beginning a Relationship with God

I tell teens, "When you choose to share the saving message of Jesus Christ with others, it can be addictive." Our ultimate goal as believers is to be like Jesus in every area of life—to carry on the ministry of Jesus Christ by sharing the gospel with others in an effort to lead them to God.

Teens who accept this challenge often are excited and confident to follow Christ's command. However, I also meet many who feel insecure and ill equipped. This is where you come in. You can be your teen's coach, adviser, and encourager as he seeks to share the faith. The first part of this task depends on his making the critical decision to receive Jesus Christ as his savior. The Bible is clear that a personal relationship with Jesus is the only way to God and to heaven (see John 14:6). How reassuring it is to know that we can't earn our way into heaven. If so, none of us would get there. Instead, we must be willing to trust our lives to Jesus for all eternity, surrendering all and believing that He will save us and change us.

Has your teen surrendered her life to Jesus? Romans 10:13 says, "Everyone who calls on the name of the Lord will be saved." Before teens can share God with others, they must first surrender their lives to Christ. To be the parent God has made you to be starts with surrendering your life, your choices, and your parenting to Him. If you or your teen has never surrendered everything to Jesus Christ, here are four steps to take. (Your teen can share these steps with others as she talks to friends about trusting Christ.)

### 1. Recognize God's Plan

God loves you and has a plan for your life. We read in the Bible, "God so loved the world that he gave his one and only Son, that whoever believes in him shall not perish but have eternal life" (John 3:16). It is God's plan that you spend eternity with Him in heaven.

### 2. Realize the Problem

Every human chooses to disobey God and do his or her own thing. The result is that we are separated from God because He is perfect and we are sinners. The Bible says, "All have sinned and fall short of the glory of God" (Romans 3:23).

### 3. Respond to God's Remedy

Because God loves you so much, He sent His Son to bridge the gap between you and Him. The gap exists because of your wrong choices. God's Son, Jesus, paid the penalty for your sins when He died on the cross and rose from the grave. The Bible says, "God demonstrates his own love for us in this: While we were still sinners, Christ died for us" (Romans 5:8).

### 4. Invite Christ into Your Life

By asking Christ to come into your life, you cross the bridge into God's family. God then forgives you and offers you a relationship with Him and the privilege of spending eternity with Him. John 1:12 says, "To all who did receive him, to those who believed in his name, he gave the right to become children of God." To receive Christ, pray a prayer such as this:

> *Dear Jesus,*
>
> *I realize I am a sinner and I need Your forgiveness. I believe that You are the Son of God and that You died for me. I want to surrender my life to You by asking You to forgive all my sins. I now invite You into my life to save me and change me and be the lord of my life. Thank You for loving me. Amen.*

If your teen has prayed this prayer for the first time, congratulations! He has made a decision that will forever change his life. Write down the date because this will be a moment you and he will never forget.

## Building a Relationship with God

The next step in equipping your teen to share Jesus is encouraging her to continue building a relationship with God. In chapter 5, I mentioned these principles that will help your teen grow in her walk with God:

1. Read and meditate on Scripture.
2. See prayer as a vital daily practice that orients one's heart to God.
3. Spend time with others who prioritize the Word and prayer.

If you haven't already, talk through these steps with your teen. His relationship with God will not develop on its own. He needs to exercise his spiritual muscles in order to grow.

Recently, I led a college football team in a pregame devotional. As I entered the weight room, I felt a bit like the Israelites facing giants. (In fact, the football players were giants!) But I loved my time with them, and I especially appreciated the words of their head coach: "These players hit it hard every day. I appreciate that you challenged them to hit it equally hard when it comes to growing in a relationship with Jesus Christ."

You are your teen's coach. I encourage you to help your whole family grow spiritually, spurring each person on in his or her relationship with God. Look for moments to stress to your teen the importance of spending time with people who are committed to prayer and God's Word. The more she hangs out with others whose faith is central in their lives, the more a faith-centric approach will be solidified in her life.

## Being Confident in a Relationship with God

"I will give you an F if you don't remove the Scripture references from your term paper!" I heard those words from my English 101 professor when I was a first-semester freshman attending a Christian college. I don't remember everything I wrote in the paper, but I do remember that the grade I received was going to be 100 percent of my grade for the course. I also remember using Scripture references several times throughout the paper to support my thesis.

But my professor was adamant that quotes from God's Word had no validity in her class. I knew that college would test my beliefs, but I never expected it to happen so soon. I didn't want to begin my college career with an F. I also knew I would be disappointed in myself if I didn't write what I believed and stand by it. I chose to keep the Bible quotes in the paper. My professor gave me a D. I wish I could tell you it was the only D I received in college (it wasn't), but it's the one I'm most proud of.

I tell teens that their beliefs will be tested. When these times come, you want your teen to be ready for the challenge. In many ways your role as a parent is all about preparing your child for such moments.

As teens choose to stand for what is right, especially their belief in who God is and what He has done for them, they need to know they will encounter pushback. Jesus warned of this in John 15:18–21:

> If the world hates you, keep in mind that it hated me first. If you belonged to the world, it would love you as its own. As it is, you do not belong to the world, but I have chosen you out of the world. That is why the world hates you. Remember what I told you: "A servant is not greater than his master." If they persecuted me, they will persecute you also. If they obeyed my teaching, they will obey yours also. They will treat you this way because of my name, for they do not know the one who sent me.

I believe that the more I stand for what is right, the more confident I become. What really jumps out at me in these verses is that the world will hate us because of our relationship with Him. Jesus went on to say, "They will put you out of the synagogue; in fact, the time is coming when anyone who kills you will think they are offering a service to God" (16:2). After telling us the world will hate us and just might kill us, Jesus ended His eye-opening challenge with these words: "I have told you these things, so that in me you may have peace. In this world you will have trouble. But take heart! I have overcome the world" (16:33).

Jesus warned us in advance about opposition in order to give us confidence. You are tasked with the same responsibility to speak such truth into the life of your teen—not to impart fear but to empower him with confidence to go to a world desperate to know the truth of who Jesus Christ is and be willing to stand firm no matter what.

## What It Looks Like to Go Public

Reading and meditating on Scripture, praying regularly, and spending time with others who do the same are vital aspects of preparing to go public with Jesus Christ. Going public means living and speaking for Jesus in a way others will understand. That's where personal faith gets real.

At the beginning of my senior year of high school, I committed to going public with God, but my first assignment didn't turn out as I'd planned. A classmate of mine and I had been enemies since junior high. I often wondered why this person didn't like me. One day he told me straight out it was because I was a Christian. So when God later told me to talk to him about what it means to be a Christian and to share my faith with him, I called him and gave the speech of my life. At the end of the call, just after giving myself a high five for a job well done, I asked my classmate if he would like to pray and receive Jesus into his life. He politely said no and then hung up. It wasn't supposed to work that way. I felt as though I had done what God asked me to, but He hadn't come through for me. I was mad at God.

I learned a lot through that experience. In particular, I learned that sharing my faith isn't just about the outcome. Regardless of how others respond, I have a responsibility to go public with God. Talking to another person about Jesus is serious stuff. As your teen commits to getting serious about living for Christ, get ready. Along with this commitment comes the responsibility to share Christ with others. The outcome, though, is always up to the Holy Spirit.

## Ready to Share

First Peter 3:15 says, "Always be ready to tell everyone who asks you why you believe as you do" (NLV). Let's say your teen is ready to go public with Christ. How can you help? In addition to sharing insights from your own experiences, here are a few steps you can take.

Help your teen write out her story of faith. A personal testimony answers these questions: Who is God to you? What did God do for you? How has God changed you? Teens don't need to have dramatic stories of turning back to God. Their stories are incredible simply because they were destined for hell and now are promised heaven.

Suggest that your teen make a list of people with whom he desires to share Jesus. Your family can then start praying for God to provide opportunities to share Jesus with these people. What a great family prayer focus!

Help your teen prepare what she is going to say. Questions can be an excellent way to begin a conversation about God, such as "What do you believe about God?" and "What confuses you the most about God?" Remind her that while one conversation might be all it takes to bring a friend to Jesus, usually it calls for patience and times of extended prayer.

Pray that God will create an opportunity and that He will give your teen boldness and the right words to say. God will bring honor to Himself no matter the outcome.

## Killing the Fear

I know teens who have no fear when given the opportunity to take the stage and morph into a rock star. Other teens are fearless on an athletic field. So why is it that many teens resist sharing Jesus with others?

I think it's because many are not consistently encouraged to share their faith. Also, some teens don't realize that going public is not about carrying a Bible around or quoting Scripture. It's about a life of daily surrender to Christ. It's about embracing God's ways over the world's. It's about staring the Enemy in the face with the same intensity they take into every sports competition.

One teen said to me, "But what if someone asks me a question about God or the Bible that I don't know how to answer? Shouldn't I hold off on talking to others until I know everything about the Bible?" Satan instills fear in teens about what they don't know about God and Scripture. Encourage your teen to be honest and tell the friend that he will find an answer. Let your child know that you always will help him get the needed answers.

Sharing Jesus with others may seem overwhelming at first. As your teen commits to growing spiritually, God will reveal Himself to her in amazing ways. Fear will be replaced with fearlessness, and your teen's faith journey of surrender will become a story to share with others.

# 18

# All-In Parents Never Give Up

I was invited to go caving with a guide and a group of teens in Wisconsin. Caving (or spelunking) is an incredible rush. With helmet-mounted lights, we plunged ever more deeply into the cave. The farther we descended, the colder it became. Gradually, most of the teens stopped and made their way back to the surface. I continued exploring for several hours, until our group had dwindled to just me, two boys, and our guide, Ryan.

The farther we went, the more difficult it became. The walls closed in around us. We went from walking to kneeling to crawling to sliding on our bellies. Eventually, we reached our destination: the entrance to a cavern called the Mud Room. Our guide had been preparing us for what he described as the coolest thing he had ever seen underground. The room was approximately twelve feet by fifteen feet in size. Thick, gooey mud covered every surface, including the walls, ceiling, and floor.

There was only one problem: the opening to the Mud Room was an incredibly tight squeeze. Ryan shimmied through, expecting the rest of us to follow. But none of us moved. The hole through which Ryan had just passed was so small that each of us realized it was going to take some tricky maneuvering to slide our bodies through it safely. After much hesitation, I decided to throw in the towel. I hollered to Ryan that we would not be joining him. Ryan hollered back, "Jeffrey, you can't come this far and not come all the way."

He was right. I took a deep breath and descended into the hole, as did the two boys. The Mud Room was exactly as advertised: a small air-filled cavity in the middle of a dense mud bog. Although the room felt unsafe, I reminded myself that it had been there without incident for a long, long time.

Ryan's statement is wisdom we need when it comes to parenting. We need to take a deep breath and do whatever it takes to guide our kids through the teen years. You've come this far, so don't give up now! Parents always remain parents, long after their sons and daughters leave high school or college. Many parents experience a rocky season during the teen years, while others make it through what can be challenging years relatively unscathed.

I asked parents whose daughters and sons were well past the high school years to share their words of wisdom. Here is some of their advice:

When children rebel during the teenage years, you often hear such things as "Well, it was the parents' fault." But that's not always the case. It's true that parents play an incredible part in this battle, yet God gives all people free will, including teenagers.

We have two children, a boy and a girl, and always raised both of them to love and honor God. The girl made it through the teen years just fine. The boy had a much rougher go of it. (We are now raising our first grandchild because of one of his decisions.)

I think it's important to know that even if you do everything as well as you can as parents, your child might still make poor choices. During some of our harder years, we found great comfort in Proverbs 22:6: "Train up a child in the way he should go, and when he is old he will not depart from it" (NKJV).

I'd say we went through about eight months of absolute agony with our middle daughter. We tried everything we could think of. At least once every day, we had a full-blown heated conversation. We had contracts, agreements, lists, charts; we took her to counseling; and we prayed nonstop. Somehow all the hard work must have paid off, because she has stopped drinking now, is (mostly) back on track with the Lord, and is through her second year in arts school.

Our youngest had a hard time, particularly in his junior and senior years, when my husband did his first tour in Iraq for sixteen months. Our son seemed to fall apart then. I didn't know what to do. I think I just gave up for part of that time. But our son made friends with a Young Life sponsor at his school, which was about the only positive influence he would allow into his life during those years. He is doing much better now. After he graduated from high school, he went into the military and is a cook at a marine base near Mosul. I know it can be hard in the military, but when he writes and calls home, his tone is still tender to the things of the Lord. We're really proud of how far he's come.

Did you hear the hope in those stories? Though the path through the teen years can be challenging, your hard work almost always pays off in the end. Allow that to encourage you, no matter what challenges you may be facing in your home.

## How to Go the Distance

Your teen is exploring new territory every day. Though he may not always seek out your guidance, it's desperately needed. He relies on you for help in finishing the journey strong. Parenting is not a sprint. The journey is ongoing, for both you and him. In this final chapter I want to leave you with a few thoughts that can help you finish the race well with your teen.

### Prepare Yourself

Satan will do everything he can to convince you that following godly parenting wisdom will be a waste. He wants you to forget it as quickly as you read it.

To guard against his attacks, pray for protection over yourself and your family. Write down this passage and put it someplace where you can see it often: "The LORD will keep you from all harm—he will watch over your life; the LORD will watch over your coming and going both now and forevermore" (Psalm 121:7–8).

### Commit Yourself to Prayer

The key to it all is prayer. Parents must never take prayer for granted. It is the greatest defense we have against the one who hates our kids. I also suggest talking with your teen about some of the things you learned in this book. As you do that, let her know that you are committing these truths to prayer as you pray every day for her specifically and individually. You can't imagine the power that is conveyed to a teenager when her parent says, "I pray for you every day."

### Be Bold in Claiming Your Calling

Your teen counts on you to do everything within your power and ability to protect him. You must give it everything you have every day. You must do whatever is necessary to guide and guard your teen through these challenging years. He needs a parent who is willing to go against the flow and take bold steps to stay connected. This commitment will reach him more powerfully than anything else. Jesus left heaven and came to earth because He understood what it meant to take extreme measures to connect with those He loves. Bold parents must be willing to have their hearts tattooed with the motto "Whatever it takes is whatever it takes."

### Live in a Way That Will Attract Honor

I am not saying that if your life is not worthy of honor, a child has the right to dishonor you. The fifth commandment (see Deuteronomy 5:16) does not require that a child honor his or her parents only if they deserve it. But children are far more likely to honor parents who live lives of integrity. Follow God's command to "be careful, and watch [yourself] closely so that you do not forget the things your eyes have seen or let them fade from your heart as long as you live. Teach them to your children and to their children after them" (4:9). We don't want our children to honor us out of duty. It's far better for them to do so out of reverence for God and respect for the example we set.

### Always Seek to Know Your Teen Better

Times around the dinner table, at home or at a restaurant, are opportunities to talk about all kinds of things. The more you know about your teen, the more equipped you will be to lead her. I encourage you to look for creative ways to educate yourself on what is important to her, what her struggles are, what she finds challenging about God, how she desires to pursue God, and more. Consider grabbing dinner at one of her favorite restaurants and asking her to answer a few questions. These examples can get you started:

- Who is in your favorite band?
- If you could change one thing about your body, what would it be?
- If you could plan the perfect vacation, where would you go and what would you do?
- What is the one question you would ask God if you had the chance?
- What three things confuse or frustrate you the most about God?
- If you could change one thing about our relationship, what would you change?

If you ask the last question, prepare for the answer, knowing it may not be what you want to hear.

## Make Your Voice Known at Your Teen's School

The public and private school campuses of America constitute the leading mission field in our nation. Your teen enters a mission field every day. Be proactive so you know what is being taught in his school. Some classes, as well as some topic-focused segments during a semester, require a parent's consent before a student can participate. Call the school to find out more. Even better, visit the classroom, talk to the teacher, and request a copy of the curriculum. You have a right to review any materials, books, homework assignments, and handouts that your teen will see. After reviewing the information that will be presented in all classes, assemblies, and special presentations, you can request that he opt out of any presentations that conflict with your family's beliefs.

It is impossible to know what your teen is exposed to if you do not stay involved. Volunteer with the PTA or PTO and attend every meeting held by the school that is open to parents. Also attend games, events, theater productions, and concerts. Don't be afraid to call the school, visit a teacher, or schedule a meeting with a school counselor or principal. As you continue to ask your teen about school life, you have an opportunity to not only reinforce positive messages but also modify and correct information that contradicts the godly qualities you desire for your child.

### You Are the Parent, Not a Pal

A high school student told me she had lived with her mom since her parents divorced eight years earlier. "But now," she said, "I'm moving in with my father in another state." She explained how difficult this move would be, considering that she was a senior and would be leaving the friends she had grown up with. I asked her why such a move was necessary. She told me, "My mom lives like she is my friend. My dad lives like my dad. He lives like he loves me!"

Her mother's lack of boundaries had sent the message that this teen girl could do whatever she wanted whenever she wanted with whomever she wanted. She realized the freedom her mom gave her was taking her nowhere fast. Let your teen see you shine in your greatest role: the role of parent. Whether you are single, married, separated, or divorced, your child needs you to be the parent, not a pal.

### Speak out of Love

I am amazed at the number of teens who tell me they rarely hear the words "I love you" from a parent. Go overboard in showing your teen a love that never fails. She needs you not only to show it but also to say it every day. If your teen doesn't find love, attention, support, encouragement, and security at home, she will look elsewhere—to someone or something—for it.

Make it a daily goal to tell your teen you love him. Work hard to help him understand that nothing he might do will change your love. Welcome every conversation, feeling, question, or doubt your teen might want to share. Also let him know that every decision you make, every line you draw, and every disciplinary action you enforce is motivated by genuine love that will never fail.

## This Is Only the Beginning

Satan would have you believe that the task before you is more daunting than anything else you might ever face. He also will tell you that you can never prepare enough to succeed. But the truth is that God created you for this. The coming days, weeks, months, and years with your teen can be the richest experience of your life.

Wherever you are on the journey, realize that the responsibility of parenting is a privilege you've been given. Every day is a new opportunity to enjoy the beauty of this call to parent one of God's beloved children. Earlier we discussed the first part of John 10:10: "The thief comes only to steal and kill and destroy." Thankfully, Jesus didn't stop with this warning. He also gave us the following assurance: "I have come that they may have life, and have it to the full."

As an all-in parent of a teen, may you not only experience a God who is real and relevant for every challenge but also grow daily in your knowledge and understanding of His immeasurable love for you. Go forward. Be determined. Be fearless. And live life to the full.

# Appendix A:
# Preventing Teen Suicide

Many students I talk to say that at some point they have thought about suicide. Many teens have friends or loved ones who have committed suicide or attempted it. Suicide is a hot topic for many due to several popular big-screen movies and Netflix series. Not only that, but suicide rates have spiked in the last twelve years among children and teens between the ages of ten and seventeen.[1] I find that even teens who aren't considering suicide often are talking about it. If you have lost someone close to you to suicide, then you know the questions that quickly surface:

- What could I have done differently?
- Did I miss the warning signs?
- If I had one more chance for a conversation with the person, what would I say?

If you are concerned that your teen may be considering suicide, it is critical that the two of you talk. I have reminded you a few times of the power of your influence. This can't be overstated as it relates to the topic of suicide. The mere fact that you are reading this book states the obvious: you love your kid. So let me remind you to keep telling her exactly this! Our children need to hear repeatedly how much they mean to us. They need the assurance that comes from hearing and knowing how proud we are of them and that we can't imagine our family without them. Look for big and small ways to convey to your child how much you love her.

But what else can you do? Here are six things you can do now to combat the lie that suicide is the only option:

1. **Validate your teen's feelings.** If you believe your teen may be considering ending his life, statements such as "Pull it

together" or "Don't feel that way" are never helpful. It's critically important for you to offer your unconditional support as you empathize with his feelings. You might say something like "I understand what you're saying, and I can imagine that you are in a lot of pain." Be willing to listen without judgment and without offering solutions (at least initially).

2. **Offer to spend time together.** As I have stressed often, interacting with your teen every day is crucial to building her confidence and her trust in you. Daily interaction also helps your teen see the good life that your family has and desires to have more of. Involving her in family discussions, devotions, and decisions are ways you can convey to your teen, "Your opinion matters to our family." In addition, I advise you to set aside special one-on-one time with her if you sense she is struggling or in deep pain. When you are generous with your time and attention, you send the message that she is important and worthy of your investment.

3. **Stay involved in your teen's life.** Keeping tabs on where your teen is, who he spends time with, and who his online friends are help you monitor his habits, online conversations, and interests. Encourage your teen to throw a party or invite friends over for pizza after a Friday-night game. Get together with other parents and invite their kids to join the party. Work creatively to stay in the know about how your teen spends his time. By doing that, you let him know that you are interested in his friends and the parents of those friends. He will realize that his friends mean something to you too.

4. **Talk to your teen about suicide.** Don't believe the lie that talking to your teen about suicide will make her think about it more. The opposite is true. As I have reminded you, the first step to getting help and hope is talking. If your teen believes that you are deeply engaged in the relationship, she will feel confident enough to confide in you about her hurts, doubts, and fears.

5. **Ask for help.** It's often important to help your teen find a mental-health professional to talk to. Reinforce the fact that you aren't handing him off to someone else. Stay involved in the process. Commit to meeting regularly with the counselor yourself. Arranging for a family-counseling session may be a valuable step as well. When someone in your family is suicidal, every family member needs to know that you are in this together.

6. **Take any step necessary.** If you are concerned that your teen might attempt suicide, do not leave her alone, and call 911 immediately. Suicide must be taken seriously—always! Make sure your teen knows that you will do whatever is necessary to help her and to prevent her from committing suicide.

## Here Are the Warning Signs

How can you know if your teen is contemplating suicide? Here are warning signs you should look for:

- He talks about wanting to die or kill himself.
- She is actively looking for a way to end her life.
- He talks about feeling hopeless or having no purpose.
- She feels trapped or mentions being in unbearable pain.

- He talks about being a burden to others.
- She has increased her use of alcohol or drugs.
- He shows signs of feeling anxious or agitated or has become reckless.
- She sleeps too little or too much.
- He has withdrawn from loved ones or feels isolated.
- She shows rage or talks about seeking revenge.
- He displays extreme mood swings.[2]

Don't ignore these warning signs. Act now to get help for your teen before it's too late. If your child or someone else you know appears to be in crisis, call the National Suicide Prevention Lifeline at (800) 273-8255.

# Appendix B:
# A Special Note for Parents of Boys

Almost weekly we hear about new allegations of sexual assault in churches, on college campuses, on movie sets, and in workplaces. Nearly all of them involve a man abusing or harassing a woman. Teen girls tell me that guys regularly request nude photos from them. Why does all this seem to be so out of control? How can parents raise sons who honor Christ in their relationships with girls?

We are seeing an epidemic of men treating women with disrespect, which has resulted in the dramatic increase in sexual-assault complaints. Although girls should also take responsibility for their actions, we must train our young men and boys how to treat women. As the parent, you have a responsibility to teach your son how to respect girls. This won't happen automatically. In a culture in which disgusting and disrespectful lust-fueled images and videos are a mere click away, you can't arm your son to do what is right by remaining passive.

Here are a few thoughts for parents of boys on how to instill in your son's heart the importance of respecting every girl and woman in his life.

## It Begins with Fathers

Dads, you must take the lead. Your son watches and learns from you. If you show respect toward women, you're teaching him to respect them. Ask yourself, *What is my son learning about respect from me?* This is where it begins. How you treat your wife and speak to her will be a daily lesson for your son.

One dad told me there are two things he often does to model good behavior in front of his boys:

1. "I ask for my wife's opinion on both big and little things. Whether it is buying a car or hanging a picture, I want my boys to see that their mother's opinion matters."

2. "I speak up whenever we see a disrespectful act toward women. Whether we are watching a movie or TV or see something on the news or at the mall, I'm consistently telling my boys, 'That isn't the way a girl should be treated.'"

I also urge you to create a culture of accountability in your home. Encourage your son to hold you accountable when you trip up. Whether you are speaking to your wife or daughter with disrespect or acting in any other way that dishonors women, invite him to call you out.

## Monitor *All* Media

Allowing your son to watch *Game of Thrones* or play games such as *Grand Theft Auto, Call of Duty,* and *Counter-Strike* teaches him to glorify sex and violence, specifically violence against women. Draw a hard line against allowing any of this stuff into your home.

I remember the first time I looked at a *Playboy* magazine. I was at a friend's house. I saw things I had never seen before. I experienced sensations I'd never felt before. Today's porn is nothing like *Playboy* porn. Modern porn is hard-core, it's often violent, and it is absolutely degrading to women.

It's not enough to have one talk with your son about the dangers of porn. You need to repeatedly tell him that porn is damaging and morally wrong. Make sure he realizes that porn will teach him that women exist merely to serve as sex toys. Tell a young son that porn exists, that friends may one day try to encourage him to view it, that some people even think it's funny, and that it teaches people lies about sex and women.

## Moms Need to Get Involved Too

I vividly remember going to the grocery store with my mom when I was a boy and hearing a man screaming at someone a few aisles over. Eventually, we realized the man was fighting with a woman. I haven't forgotten my mom telling me that a man should never treat any woman in such a way. As a mom, you have a strong influence over your son. Use your insight to encourage him to never say or do anything that would disrespect a girl. Call him out if he makes a comment or tells a joke about a girl that is degrading or inappropriate.

## Teach Your Son
## the Meaning of Consent

Your son needs to know that no means no. Boys need to hear from parents about consent. When talking to your son, be detailed, specific, and clear. Tell him that he never has the right to do anything that involves a girl without her consent. This applies to holding her hand, giving her a hug or kiss, and any other action that involves touching her. It also means not taking her to a place she doesn't want to go or pressuring her to change her mind if she has said no to any of these things.

Talk about scenarios your son might find himself in at a party or on a date. Speak clearly about striving for purity, honoring God, and doing what is right regardless of what merely *feels* right in the moment. This is a conversation you need to have over and over with him.

## Use Scripture in Teachable Moments

As I have suggested throughout this book, integrate the Bible into everyday conversations with your son. Read verses that focus on integrity and respect. For example, use the Old Testament story of when King David lusted after a married woman, had sex with her, got her pregnant, tried to cover it up, had her husband killed in battle, and then took the man's widow to be his own wife. Talk about how it all went wrong for David and discuss how he could have acted differently.

Be a great example for your son in how you live and in the conversations you have. Remember, our kids follow our lead, so let's give them godly examples of lives worth following.

# Acknowledgments

Thank you to the entire Multnomah team, especially to my editor, Ingrid Beck. Thank you for your wisdom and commitment to this project. Thank you also to Kathy Mosier for an amazing edit.

Thank you to the many who have supported Jeffrey Dean Ministries and prayed for our outreach. We have been able to share truth with so many because you prayed.

Mom and Dad, thank you for leading the way as parents. I am so honored to be your son and to have watched you model the love of Christ to our family and friends all these years.

To my wife, Amy, you are my best friend, and I love you and our life together. Thank you for teaching me to be a better husband and father.

To Bailey and Brynnan, it is a blast every day to be your daddy. Thank you for innumerable laughs and hugs. I pray that you both will follow Jesus Christ all your lives. Mommy and I love you both.

To Mike and Kim Blackwood, you have been with us every step of the way. Thank you for long talks and even longer prayers. Amy and I love you.

To parents everywhere who are working hard every day to raise successful teens: never stop.

## Chapter 2: Reality Is Hard, but You Have the Advantage

1. *Strong's Concordance Greek Lexicon,* s.v. "kléptēs," www.messie 2vie.fr/bible/strongs/strong-greek-G2812-kleptes.html.

2. *The KJV New Testament Greek Lexicon,* s.v. "thuo," www.bible studytools.com/lexicons/greek/kjv/thuo.html.

3. William White, "5 Top Trends for Teenagers 2017," Investor Place, April 11, 2017, https://investorplace.com/2017/04/top-trends -for-teenagers.

4. Mike Nappa, *The Jesus Survey: What Christian Teens Really Believe and Why* (Ada, MI: Baker, 2012), 11.

5. Dan Roberts and Sabrina Siddiqui, "Gay Marriage Declared Legal Across the US in Historic Supreme Court Ruling," *Guardian,* June 26, 2015, www.theguardian.com/society/2015/jun/26/gay -marriage-legal-supreme-court.

6. Chiara Sabina, Janis Wolak, and David Finkelhor, "The Nature and Dynamics of Internet Pornography Exposure for Youth," *Cyber Psychology & Behavior* 11, no. 6 (2008), www.unh.edu /ccrc/pdf/CV169.pdf.

7. Associated Press, "Study: More Kids Exposed to Online Porn," Children's Health on NBCNews.com, February 5, 2007, www .nbcnews.com/id/16981028/ns/health-childrens_health/t/study -more-kids-exposed-online-porn/#.WtSxgS-ZMvo.

8. Maggie Jones, "What Teenagers Are Learning from Online Porn," *New York Times Magazine,* February 7, 2018, www.nytimes.com /2018/02/07/magazine/teenagers-learning-online-porn-literacy-sex -education.html.

## Chapter 4: Focusing on What Matters Most

1. "A Measure of Salt," NASA Earth Observatory, June 11, 2012, https://earthobservatory.nasa.gov/images/78250/a-measure-of-salt.
2. Marissa Laliberte, "America's Favorite Ice Cream Flavor Isn't Chocolate or Vanilla," Business Insider, August 14, 2017, www .businessinsider.com/americas-favorite-ice-cream-flavor-isnt -chocolate-or-vanilla-2017-8.
3. "Do Babies Have Kneecaps?," DocCheck News, March 3, 2017, http://news.doccheck.com/en/blog/post/5750-do-babies-have -kneecaps.
4. Fred Hosier, "33,000 Injured Each Year While Using the Toilet," Safety News Alert, August 22, 2011, www.safetynewsalert.com /33000-injured-each-year-while-using-the-toilet.

## Chapter 6: The Critical Role of a Father

1. *The Princess Bride,* directed by Rob Reiner (Los Angeles: Twentieth Century Fox, 1987). The story is based on a book and screenplay; see William Goldman, *The Princess Bride* (New York: Ballantine /Del Rey, 1974, 1992), 111.
2. "Conflict Resolution," loveisrespect.org, www.loveisrespect.org /healthy-relationships/conflict-resolution.

## Chapter 9: Getting the Most out of Dinnertime

1. *Field of Dreams,* directed by Phil Alden Robinson (Universal City, CA: Universal Pictures, 1989).

## Chapter 10: Navigating Our Media-Driven World

1. Nigel Edelshain, "Young People Still Read Print Magazines," *Wainscot* (blog), June 25, 2017, http://wainscotmedia.com/blog /young-people-still-read-print-magazines.

## Chapter 11: Setting Healthy Boundaries for Cell Phone Usage

1. Merriam-Webster, s.v. "sexting," www.merriam-webster.com /dictionary/sexting.

2. Darian Somers, "Do Colleges Look at Your Social Media Accounts?," *U.S. News & World Report,* February 10, 2017, www .usnews.com/education/best-colleges/articles/2017-02-10/colleges -really-are-looking-at-your-social-media-accounts.

3. Lauren Salm, "70% of Employers Are Snooping Candidates' Social Media Profiles," Career Builder, June 15, 2017, www.careerbuilder .com/advice/social-media-survey-2017.

4. Mel Judson, "25 Unbelievable (SFW) Facts About the 'Adult Industry,'" Ranker, www.ranker.com/list/porn-industry-secrets /mel-judson.

5. Judson, "25 Unbelievable (SFW) Facts."

6. Judson, "25 Unbelievable (SFW) Facts."

7. Judson, "25 Unbelievable (SFW) Facts."

8. Ashley Fowler, "Anal Sex: From Stigma and Myths to Facts," Sex, Etc., July 31, 2017, https://sexetc.org/info-center/post/anal-sex -stigma-and-myths-to-facts.

9. "Do I Need to Use Protection During Oral Sex?," Sex, Etc., https:// sexetc.org/info-center/post/do-i-need-to-use-protection-during -oral-sex.

10. "After Becoming Pregnant How Long Is Too Long to Wait Before You Have an Abortion? Is It Possible to Get an Abortion After the First Trimester?," Sex, Etc., https://sexetc.org/info-center/post /after-becoming-pregnant-how-long-is-too-long-to-wait-before -you-have-an-abortion-is-it-possible-to-get-an-abortion-after-the -first-trimester.

11. "Videos, Quizzes, and Games," Planned Parenthood, www .plannedparenthood.org/learn/teens/tools-for-teens.

12. Perri Klass, "Teenagers Are Sexting—Now What?," *New York Times,* March 12, 2018, www.nytimes.com/2018/03/12/well /family/teens-are-sexting-now-what.html.

## Chapter 12: What to Do About Pornography

1. "Pornography Statistics," Covenant Eyes, www.covenanteyes.com /pornstats.

2. "20 Mind-Blowing Stats About the Porn Industry and Its Underage Consumers," Fight the New Drug, January 3, 2019, https://fightthenewdrug.org/10-porn-stats-that-will-blow-your -mind.

3. *Pornography Statistics: 250+ Facts, Quotes, and Statistics About Pornography Use (2015 Edition),* Covenant Eyes, 14, www .covenanteyes.com/lemonade/wp-content/uploads/2013/02 /2015-porn-stats-covenant-eyes.pdf.

4. Bethany Brookshire, "Dopamine Is _____: Is It Love? Gambling? Reward? Addiction?," *Slate,* July 3, 2013, https://slate.com /technology/2013/07/what-is-dopamine-love-lust-sex-addiction -gambling-motivation-reward.html.

## Chapter 13: Talking with Your Teen About Dating

1. Jamie Ducharme, "Teens Are 'Juuling' at School. Here's What That Means," *Time,* March 27, 2018, http://time.com/5211536 /what-is-juuling.

2. Raychelle Cassada Lohmann, "Teen Dating Violence: What Parents and Teens Should Know," *U.S. News & World Report,* February 21, 2017, https://health.usnews.com/wellness/for-parents

/articles/2017-02-21/teen-dating-violence-what-parents-and-teens
-should-know.

3. Emily F. Rothman et al., "The Proportion of US Parents Who
Talk with Their Adolescent Children About Dating Abuse,"
*Journal of Adolescent Health* 49, no. 2 (August 2011): 216–18,
www.jahonline.org/article/S1054-139X(11)00164-9/abstract
?code=jah-site.

### Appendix A: Preventing Teen Suicide

1. Jayne O'Donnell and Anne Saker, "Teen Suicide Is Soaring. Do
Spotty Mental Health and Addiction Treatment Share Blame?,"
*USA Today,* March 19, 2018, www.usatoday.com/story/news
/politics/2018/03/19/teen-suicide-soaring-do-spotty-mental
-health-and-addiction-treatment-share-blame/428148002.

2. "Warning Signs of Suicide," SAVE: Suicide Awareness Voices
of Education, https://save.org/about-suicide/warning-signs-risk
-factors-protective-factors.

# Connect with Jeffrey Dean and Learn More About His Ministry

Web: jeffreydean.com

Podcast: *Family Strong with Jeffrey Dean*

 @iamjeffreydean

 @iamjeffreydean

 @iamjeffreydean

# More Books from Jeffrey Dean

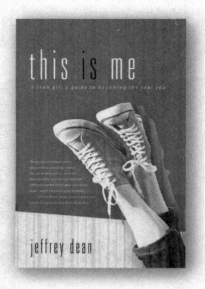

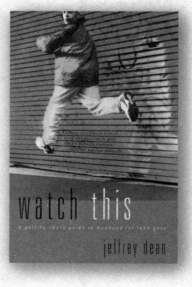